LEVEL ONE

D1865111

David Carr Glover METHOD for PIANO

LESSONS

David Carr Glover
and Jay Stewart

Design and illustrations: Jeannette Aquino
Editor: Carole Flatau

FOREWORD

Teacher and Parents:

LESSONS, Level One, from the David Carr Glover METHOD for PIANO reviews the basic concepts presented in LESSONS, Primer Level. New concepts are introduced and reinforced sequentially through the use of original compositions, folk songs and the sounds of today. This book, combined with the recommended supplementary materials, continues to assist the student in developing the ability to read and perform musically through interval recognition, sight reading and ear training.

The student will continue to experience the basic elements of improvisation as the creative activities, EXPLORE, are presented.

Supplementary materials are carefully correlated and coded with the LESSONS book to provide reinforcement of all concepts.

The David Carr Glover METHOD for PIANO has been created to provide an enjoyable program of piano instruction which is pedagogically sound. David Carr Glover and his collaborators wish you a happy, successful musical journey!

Supplementary materials correlated with
LESSONS, Level One, from the
David Carr Glover METHOD for PIANO

THEORY .... Introduce with Page 4

SIGHT READING AND EAR TRAINING .... Page 8

TECHNIC .... Page 10

PERFORMANCE .... Page 11

Additional teaching aids include
Music Assignment Book, Music Flash Cards,
Manuscript Writing Book

Contents

Music Fundamentals - Reference and Review

THE GRAND STAFF

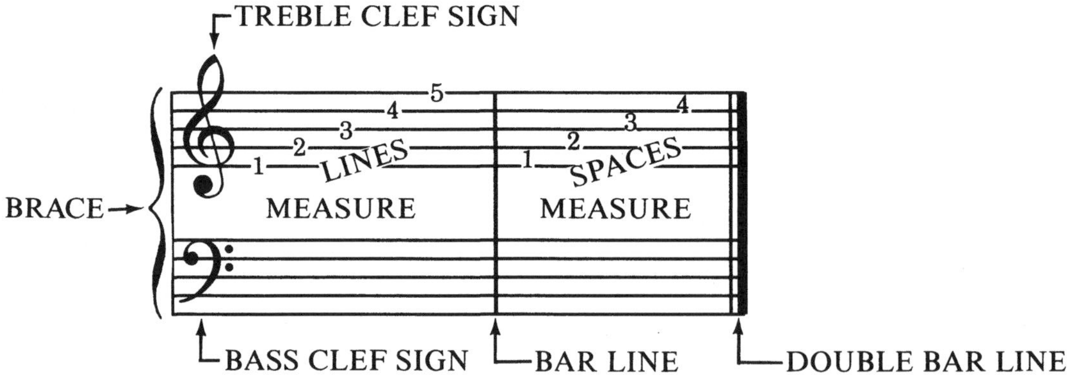

KEY - NOTE CHART

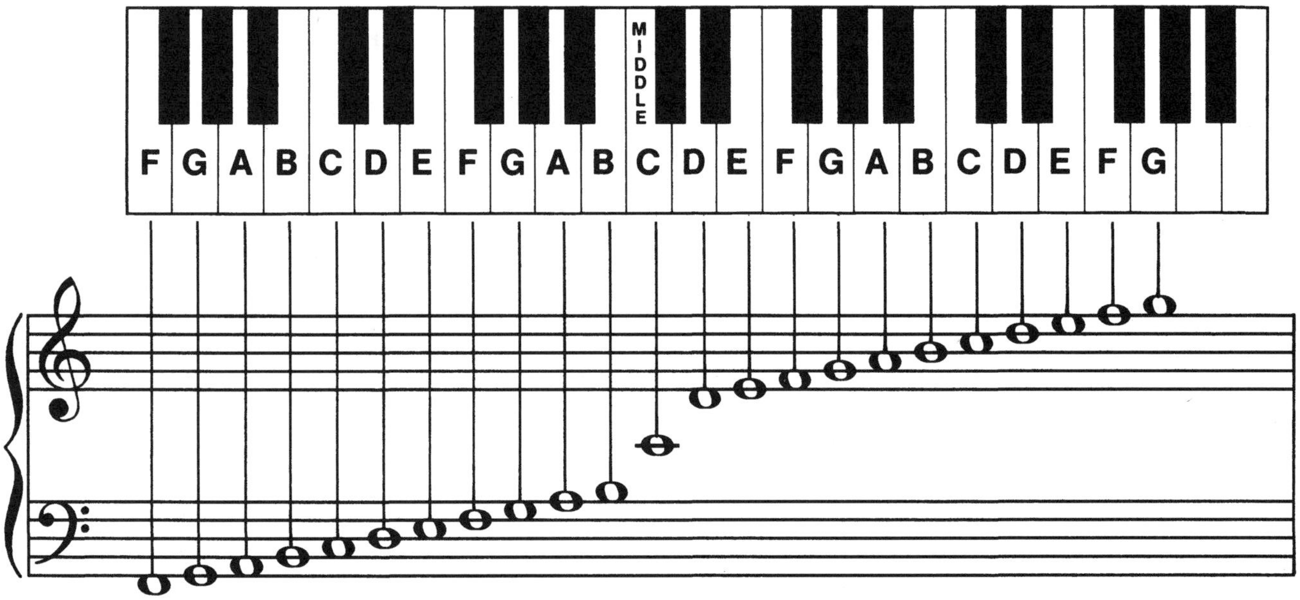

TIME SIGNATURES

2 → Beats to a measure
4 → Each quarter note receives one beat

3 → Beats to a measure
4 → Each quarter note receives one beat

4 → Beats to a measure
4 → Each quarter note receives one beat

NOTE AND REST VALUES

Quarter Note	= 1 beat
Half Note	= 2 beats
Dotted Half Note	= 3 beats
Whole Note	= 4 beats

Quarter Rest	= 1 beat
Half Rest	= 2 beats
Whole Measure Rest	= 3 beats (3/4 time)
Whole Measure Rest	= 4 beats (4/4 time)

You are now ready for THEORY, Level One, of the David Carr Glover METHOD for PIANO.

Music Terms

f (forte) — Play loudly.

p (piano) — Play softly.

Legato — Play smoothly and connected.

Slur  A curved line over or under a group of notes. Play legato.

Phrase — A musical thought or sentence, usually played legato.

Tie 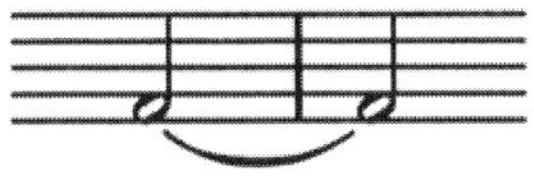 A curved line joining two notes on the same line or space. Play the first note and let it sound for the value of both notes.

♭ — Flat sign. Play the next key DOWN to the LEFT.

♯ — Sharp sign. Play the next key UP to the RIGHT.

Staccato  Play the note detached, not connected.

INTERVALS

The distance from one tone to another is called an interval.
Numbers are used to name intervals.

2nds 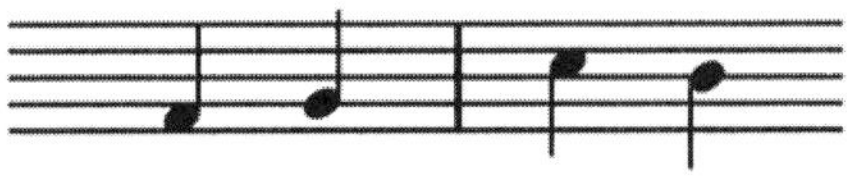 from a line note to the next space note, or from a space note to the next line note

3rds 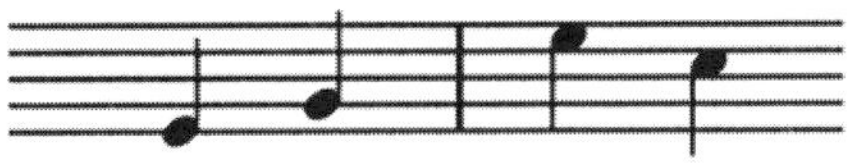 from a line note to the next line note, or from a space note to the next space note

4ths 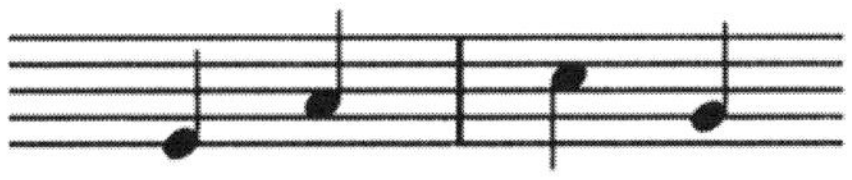 from a line note to a space note, or from a space note to a line note

5ths 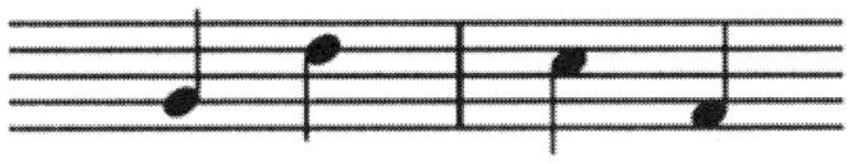 from a line note to a line note, or from a space note to a space note

POSITION (Review)

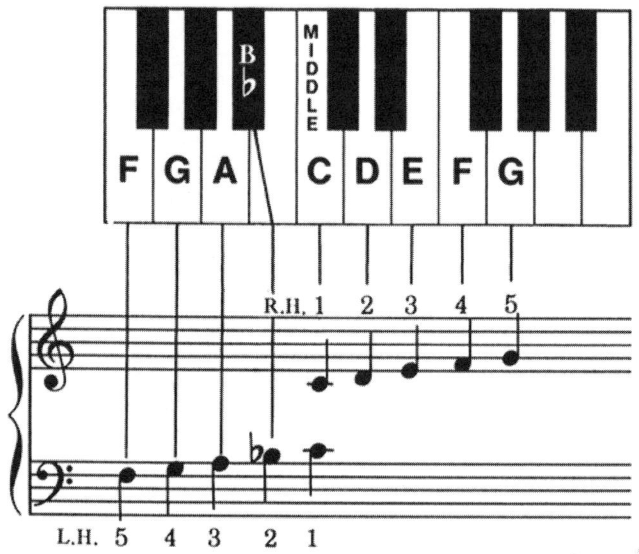

THIS OLD MAN

TRADITIONAL

Second part (Student plays solo one octave higher.)

Stems up - R.H.
Stems down - L.H.

POSITION (Review)

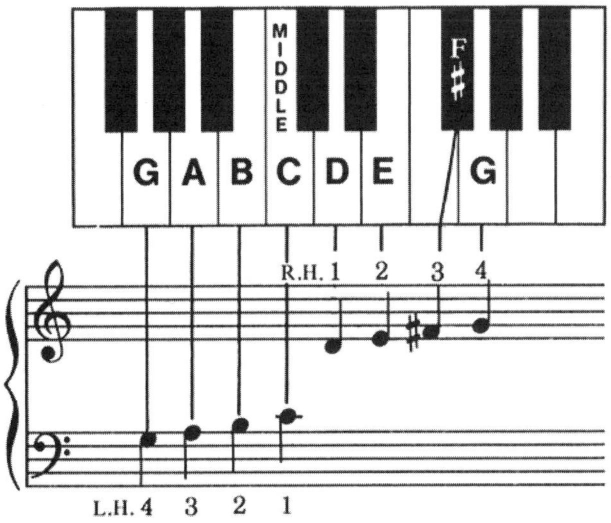

I'M A LITTLE TEAPOT

TRADITIONAL

HALF STEPS - WHOLE STEPS

The keyboard has HALF STEPS and WHOLE STEPS. From one key to the very next key is a Half Step. From one key to another key with one key in between is a Whole Step.

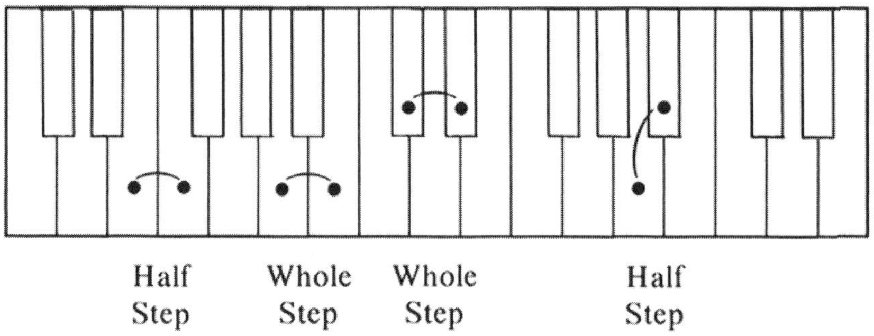

Under the marked keys write H for Half Steps and W for Whole Steps.

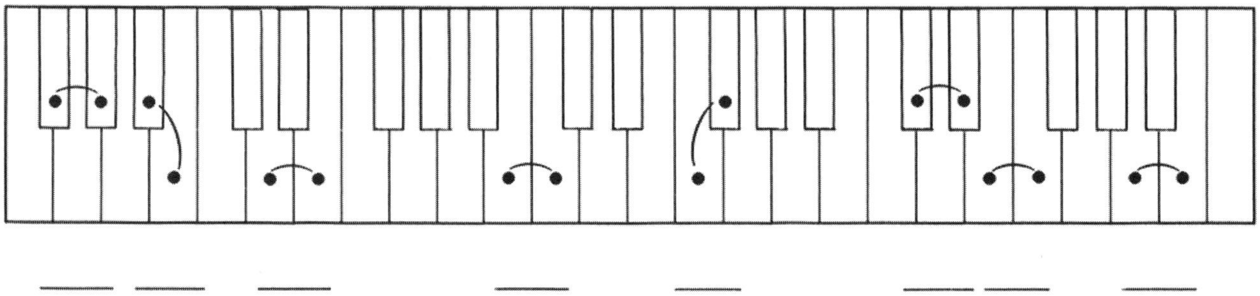

SHARPS - FLATS

When a sharp sign ♯ appears before a note, the note is **raised** one half step.
When a flat sign ♭ appears before a note, the note is **lowered** one half step.
Sharps and flats are called ACCIDENTALS when they do not appear in the key signature. (Key signatures will be presented on page 19.)

Under the following pairs of notes write H for half steps and W for whole steps.

The notes that form the C Major Five Finger Position create a pattern of half and whole steps all on the white keys.

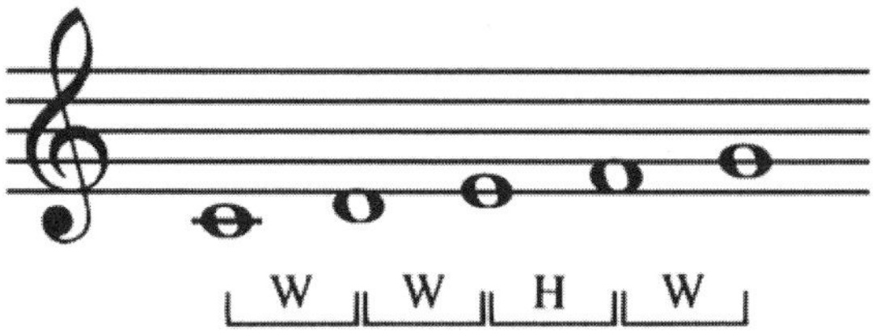

You are now ready for SIGHT READING AND EAR TRAINING, Level One, of the David Carr Glover METHOD for PIANO.

Key of C Major *

C MAJOR POSITION (Review)

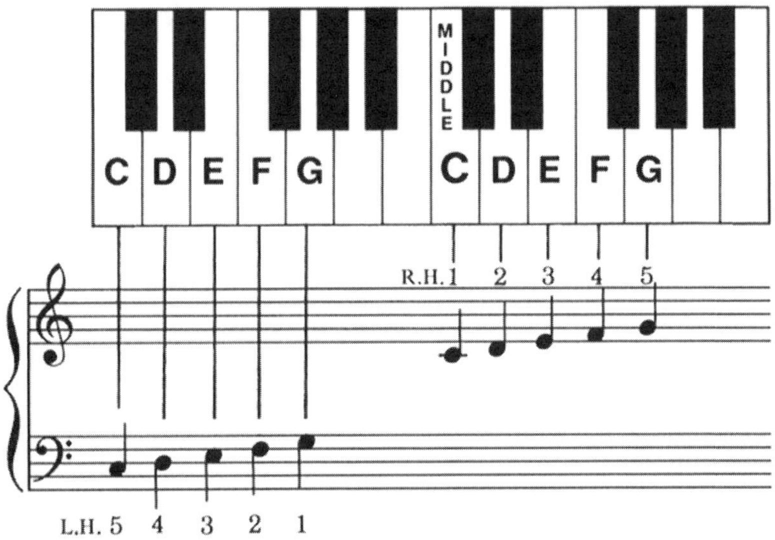

DIRECTIONS:

1. Before playing, clap and count the rhythm aloud.
2. Find the correct position for both hands on the keyboard.
3. Keep your eyes on the music as you play.
4. Play and count aloud.
5. Play and sing the words.

ALWAYS practice SLOWLY to play the correct fingering, notes, rhythm and expression as you begin learning a piece.
The speed may then be gradually increased.

FOLLOW THESE DIRECTIONS FOR EACH PIECE IN THIS BOOK!

Student: Explain the 4/4 time signature.

TAKE IT EASY

*Key signatures will be introduced on page 19.

Reviewing Intervals

An INTERVAL is the distance between two tones. To identify intervals, count the number of the lines and spaces between the two notes, including the lowest and highest notes forming the interval. ALWAYS count from the bottom note to the top note.

HARMONIC AND MELODIC INTERVALS

When intervals are played this way

they are called MELODIC INTERVALS.
Each note is played separately.

When intervals are played this way

they are called HARMONIC INTERVALS.
The notes are played together.

Notes played separately form a MELODY.
Two or more notes played together make HARMONY.

1. Draw these intervals next to each given example.

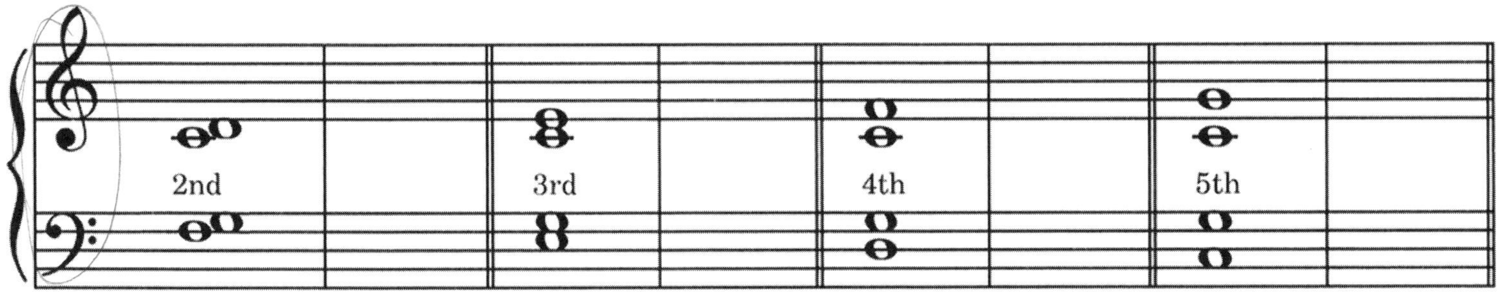

2. LISTEN carefully to the sounds of these melodic and harmonic intervals as you play and say their number names.

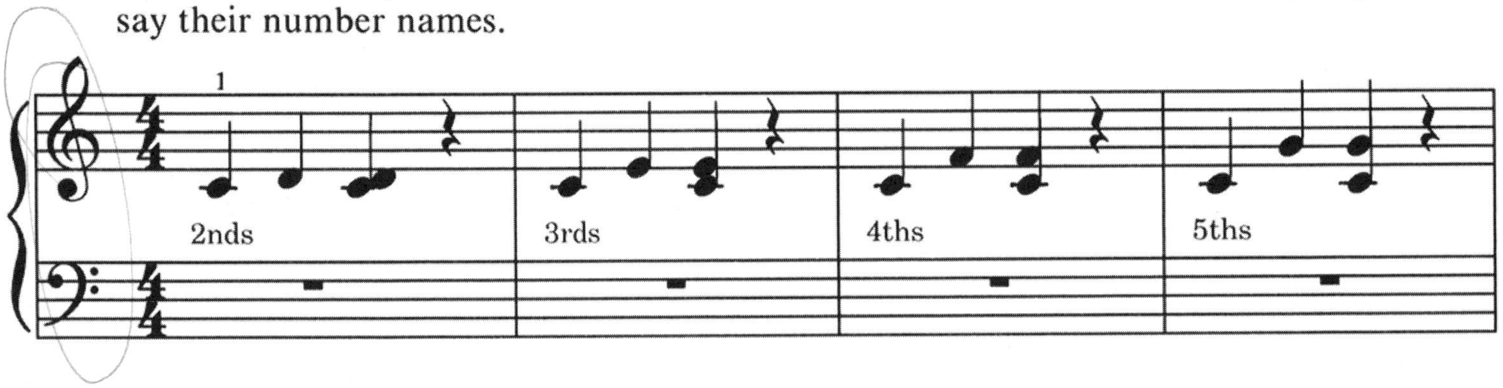

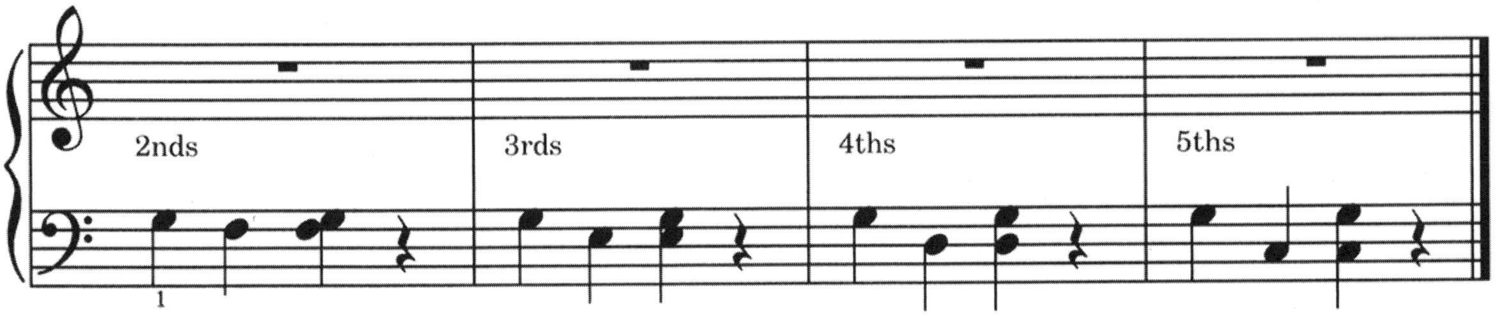

You are now ready for TECHNIC, Level One, of the David Carr Glover METHOD for PIANO.

First Ending

1. Play first time only, then repeat the section.

Second Ending

2. Play second time, skipping the first ending.

Practice this interval accompaniment before playing "Row Your Boat". Keep your eyes on the music. Do not look at your hands.

Repeat sign (Go back to the beginning and play again.)

Student: Explain the $\frac{3}{4}$ time signature.

mp	- mezzo piano - moderately soft
mf	- mezzo forte - moderately loud

ROW YOUR BOAT

TRADITIONAL

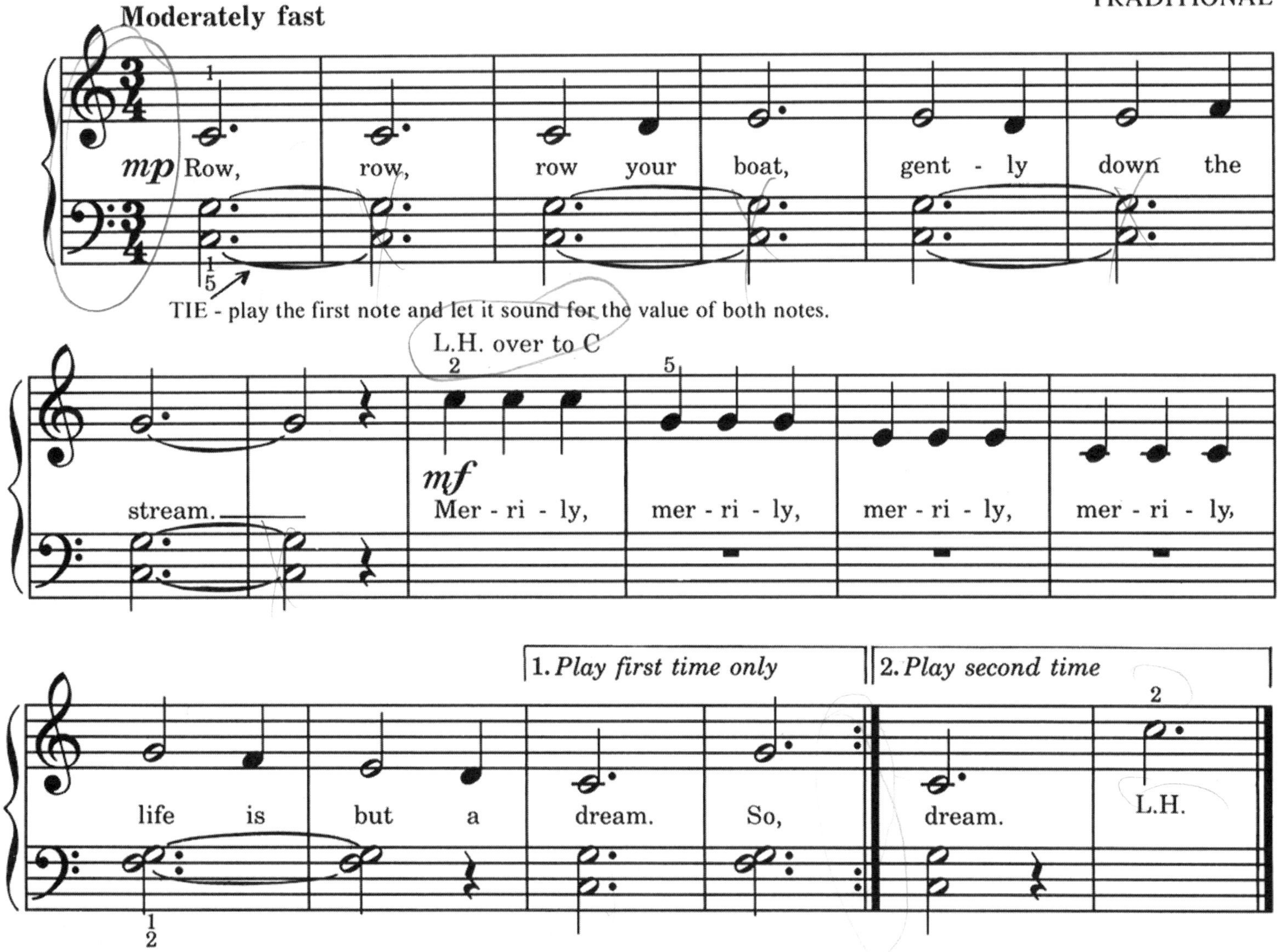

EXPLORE: With both hands, tap the rhythm of this piece.

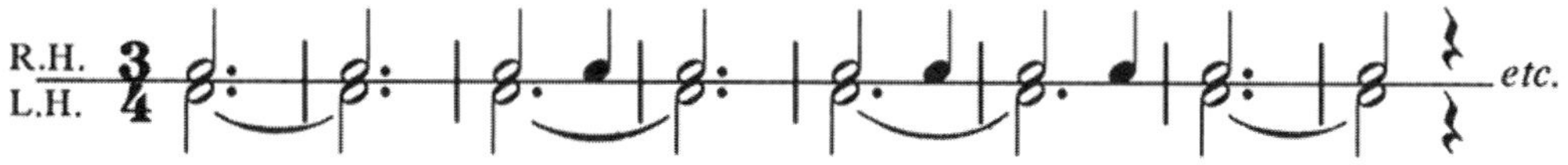

Do this activity with many other pieces in this book.

You are now ready for PERFORMANCE, Level One, of the David Carr Glover METHOD for PIANO.

TEMPO, an Italian word, means rate of speed. TEMPO MARKS are Italian or English words used to indicate the rate of speed for a piece. They are placed at the beginning of a piece. The TEMPO for "Go Tell Aunt Rhodie" is Moderato, meaning a moderate speed.

Tempo Marks

ADAGIO	ANDANTE	MODERATO	ALLEGRETTO	ALLEGRO
Slow, at leisure	Slow, gentle, walking tempo	Moderately	Moderately fast	Fast, cheerful

GO TELL AUNT RHODIE

TRADITIONAL

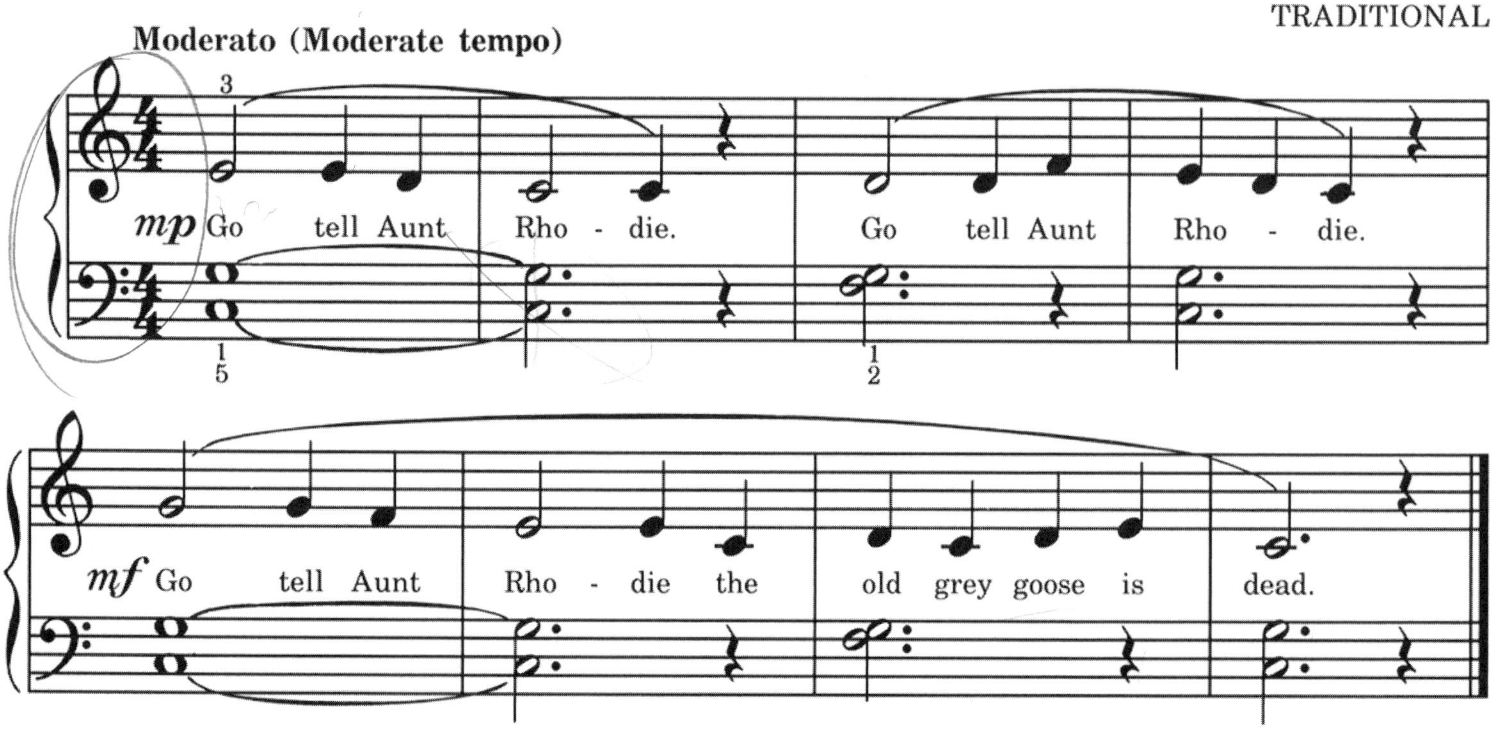

EXPLORE: Change the mood of this piece. Play all the Es as E flats.

RITARDANDO means to gradually slow the tempo. *Rit.* is its abbreviation.
A Tempo means to resume the original tempo.

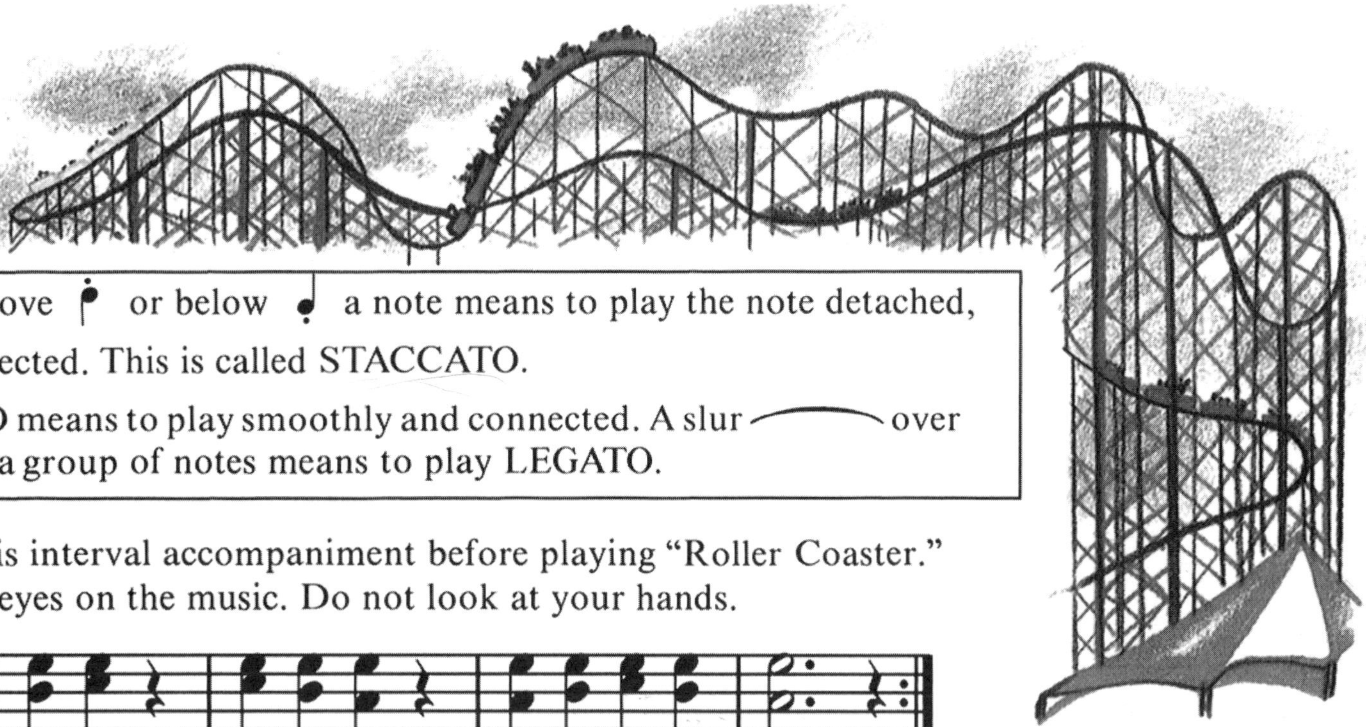

A dot above or below a note means to play the note detached, not connected. This is called STACCATO.

LEGATO means to play smoothly and connected. A slur over or under a group of notes means to play LEGATO.

Practice this interval accompaniment before playing "Roller Coaster." Keep your eyes on the music. Do not look at your hands.

ROLLER COASTER

GLOVER - STEWART

UPBEAT

One or more notes may appear BEFORE the complete measure of a piece.
These notes are called the UPBEAT.
The remaining beats of the first INCOMPLETE MEASURE are usually found in the last measure of the piece.

What does Allegro mean? ____________

WHEN THE SAINTS GO MARCHING IN

TRADITIONAL

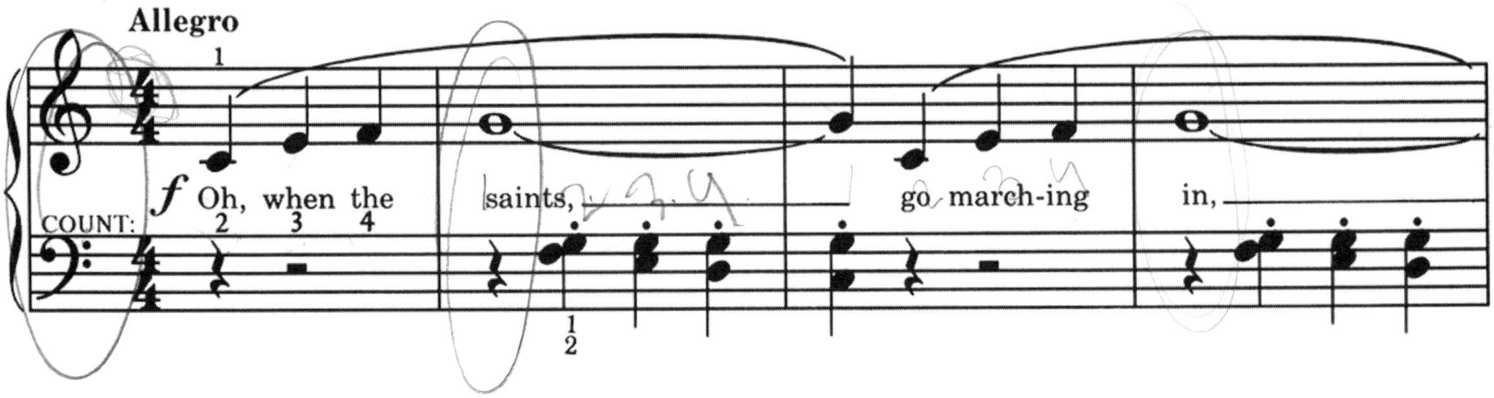

Second Part (Student plays solo one octave higher.)

EXPLORE: CHALLENGE! Play **all** the left hand notes (even the whole and half notes) with a quarter note pulse.

Oh, when the saints go march - ing in,
How I want to be there with them
When the saints go march - ing in.

MIDDLE C POSITION

(Review)

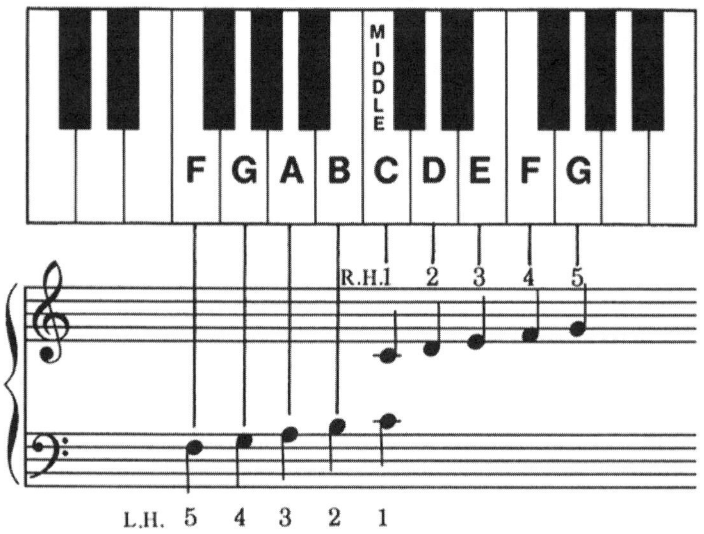

Aaron Copland (1900 -), an American composer, has appeared as a pianist and conductor throughout the world. He has been granted many prestigious awards and prizes for his compositions.

"The Gift to Be Simple" is a lovely traditional folk tune used by Aaron Copland in his famous composition, *Appalachian Spring.*

THE GIFT TO BE SIMPLE

TRADITIONAL

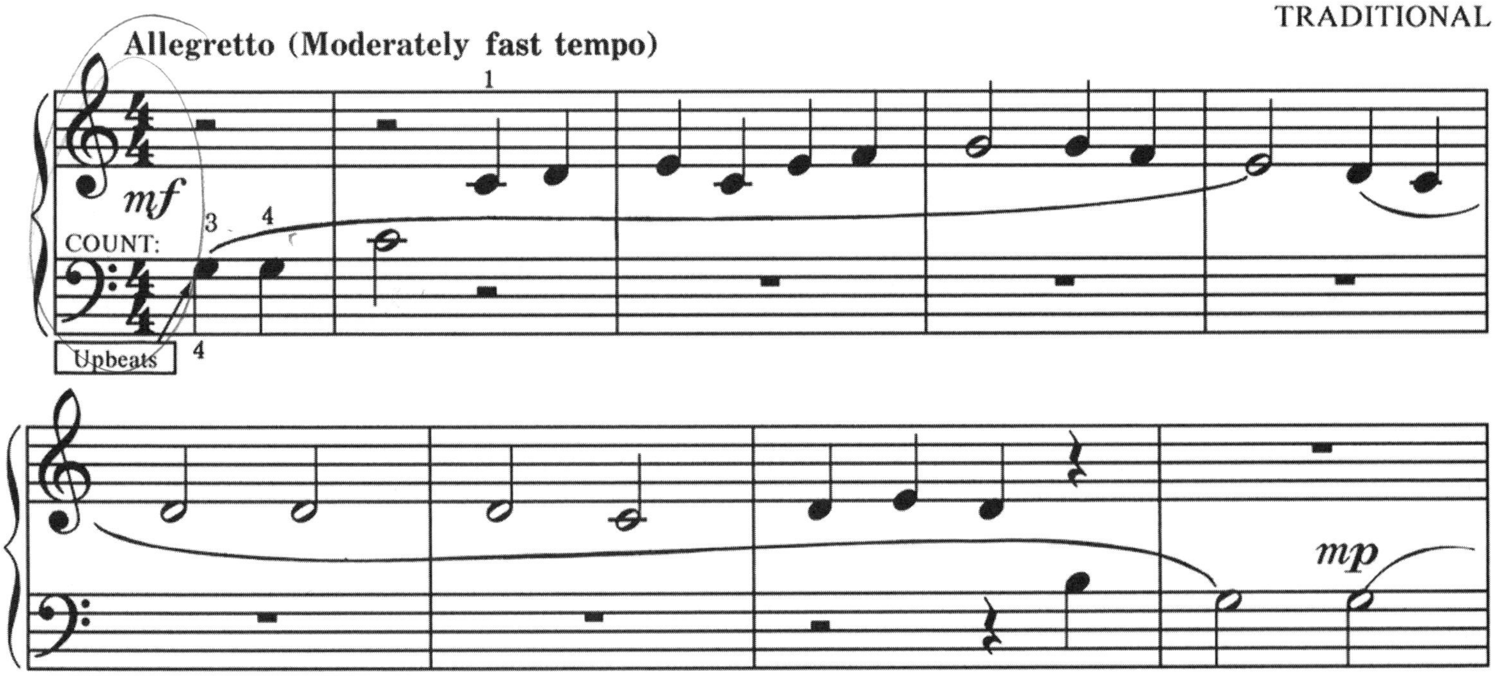

Second Part (Student plays solo one octave higher.)

rit.

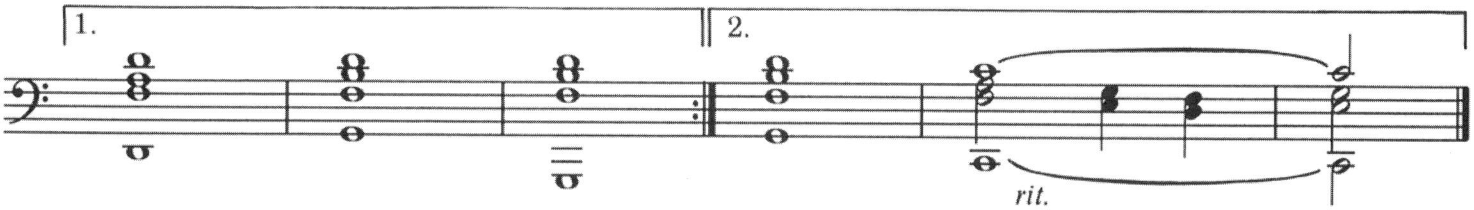
1.
2.
rit.

TONE BALANCE

One hand will often play louder than the other. This is called TONE BALANCE.

In the following solo the left hand creates the melody and is played louder than the accompaniment played by the right hand.

What does Moderato mean? ___________

MERRY-GO-ROUND

GLOVER - STEWART

EXPLORE: Make the sound of a *broken* merry-go-round. Play the left hand as written. In the right hand change all the Fs to F sharps.

Reviewing

HALF STEPS - WHOLE STEPS

Under the marked keys write H for half steps and W for whole steps.

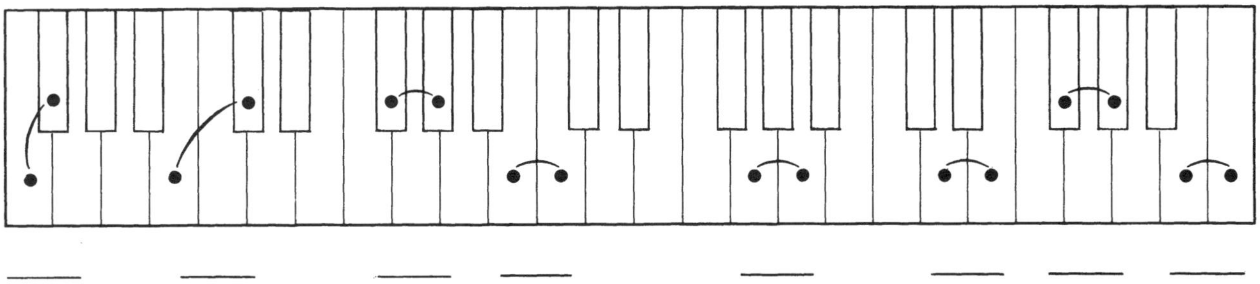

Under the following pairs of notes write H for half steps and W for whole steps.

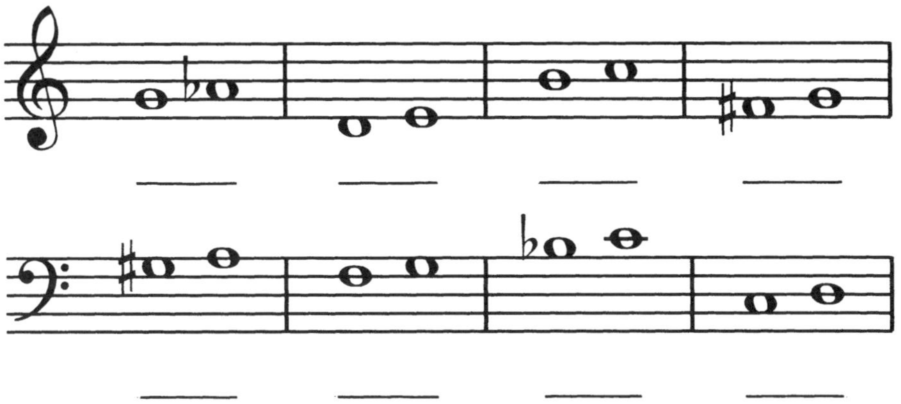

The notes that form the G Major Five Finger Position create a pattern of half and whole steps.

IMPORTANT: Notice that although the notes for the G Major Five Finger Position are different from the C Major Five Finger Position, the half and whole step pattern is the same.

KEY OF G MAJOR

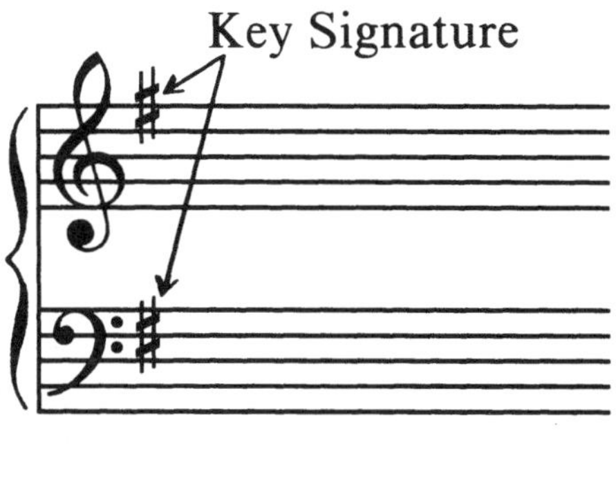

The key of G Major has one sharp, F♯ , placed at the beginning of each staff. This means all Fs are to be played sharp. This is called the KEY SIGNATURE.

(The key of C Major has no sharps or flats.)

Key of G Major

NEW G MAJOR POSITION

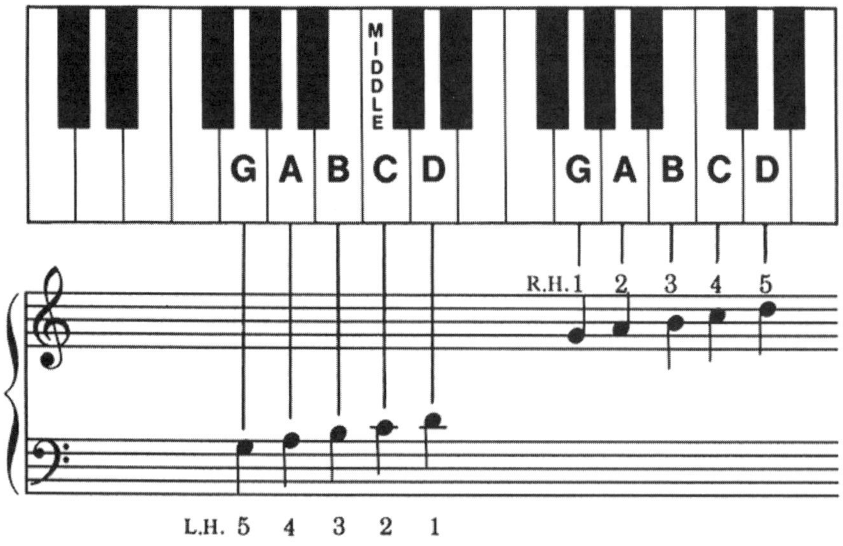

IMPORTANT: The G Major Five Finger Position does not include the note F♯.

Key of ________, Key signature ________

GEE, THAT'S EASY

GLOVER - STEWART

DYNAMIC SIGNS

DYNAMIC SIGNS are placed in music to help the performer with musical expression.

Crescendo *(cresc.)* means to play gradually louder.

Diminuendo *(dim.)* means to play gradually softer.

What does Allegretto mean? ____________

SNOWFLAKES

GLOVER - STEWART

EXPLORE: Change the mood of this piece. Play all the Bs as B flats.

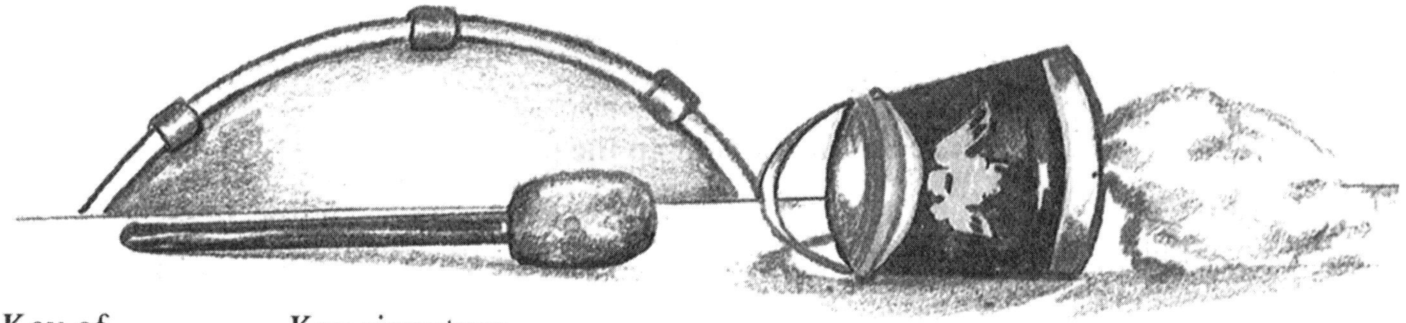

Key of ________. Key signature ________.

PARADE

GLOVER - STEWART

EXPLORE: Play the left hand accompaniment of this piece as you sing the melody. (Sing the words or note names.) DO NOT play the right hand.
For excellent ear training, do this activity with other pieces in this book.

FERMATA SIGN

This sign 𝄐 is called a FERMATA. It means to hold the note or rest longer than the given time value.

Practice this interval accompaniment before playing "Lullaby."
Keep your eyes on the music. Do not look at your hands.

LULLABY

D.C. al fine is the abbreviation for Da Capo al Fine.
It means return to the beginning and play to the word *Fine* (pronounced fee-nay).
The dots inside the double bars indicate that all music between the double bars is to be repeated.

ACCENT MARK >

This > is an ACCENT MARK. When the ACCENT is placed over or under a note, it means to play that note LOUDER.

Practice this interval accompaniment before playing "What's For Dinner?" Keep your eyes on the music. Do not look at your hands.

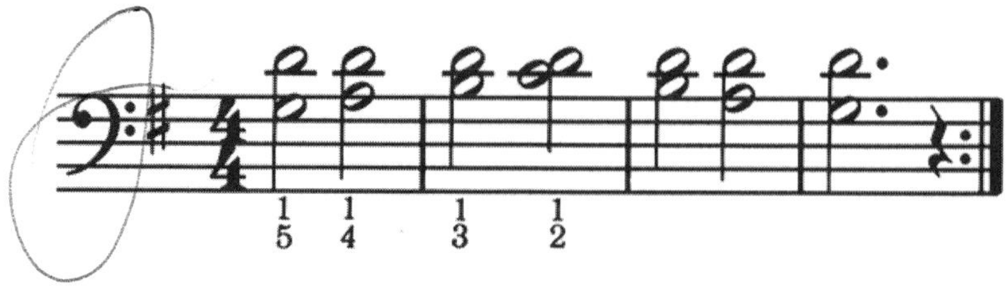

WHAT'S FOR DINNER?

Allegretto

GLOVER - STEWART

EXPLORE: With both hands, tap the rhythm of this piece.

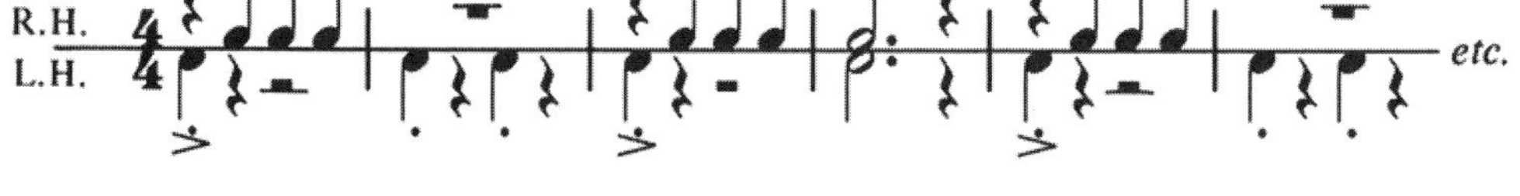

Do this activity with many other pieces in this book.

Eighth Note and Eighth Rest

This is an EIGHTH NOTE. It receives ½ a beat when the quarter note receives one beat.

Two or more eighth notes may be written like this:

Two eighth notes = one quarter note and receive one beat in 2/4, 3/4 and 4/4 time.

This is an EIGHTH REST. It has the same time value as one eighth note.

Clap and count aloud the following rhythm pattern.

Count:	4	&	1	&	2	&	3	&	4	&	1	&	2	&	3	&	4	&	1	&	2	&	3	&	4	&	1	&	2	&	3	&						
or:	4	a	1	a	2	a	3	a	4	a	1	a	2	a	3	a	4	a	1	a	2	a	3	a	4	a	1	a	2	a	3	a						
or:	4-or		1-un		2-oo		3-ee		4-or		1-un		2-oo		3-ee		4-or		1-un		2-oo		3-ee		4-or		1-un		2-oo		3-ee							

Your teacher will tell you which way to count.

Play and count aloud SLOWLY, "Rise and Shine."
TEACHER: Clap a quarter note pulse as student plays and counts.

RISE AND SHINE

TRADITIONAL

G MAJOR POSITION
(Review)

Student: Explain the $\frac{2}{4}$ time signature.

KEY OF G WITH EASE, PLEASE

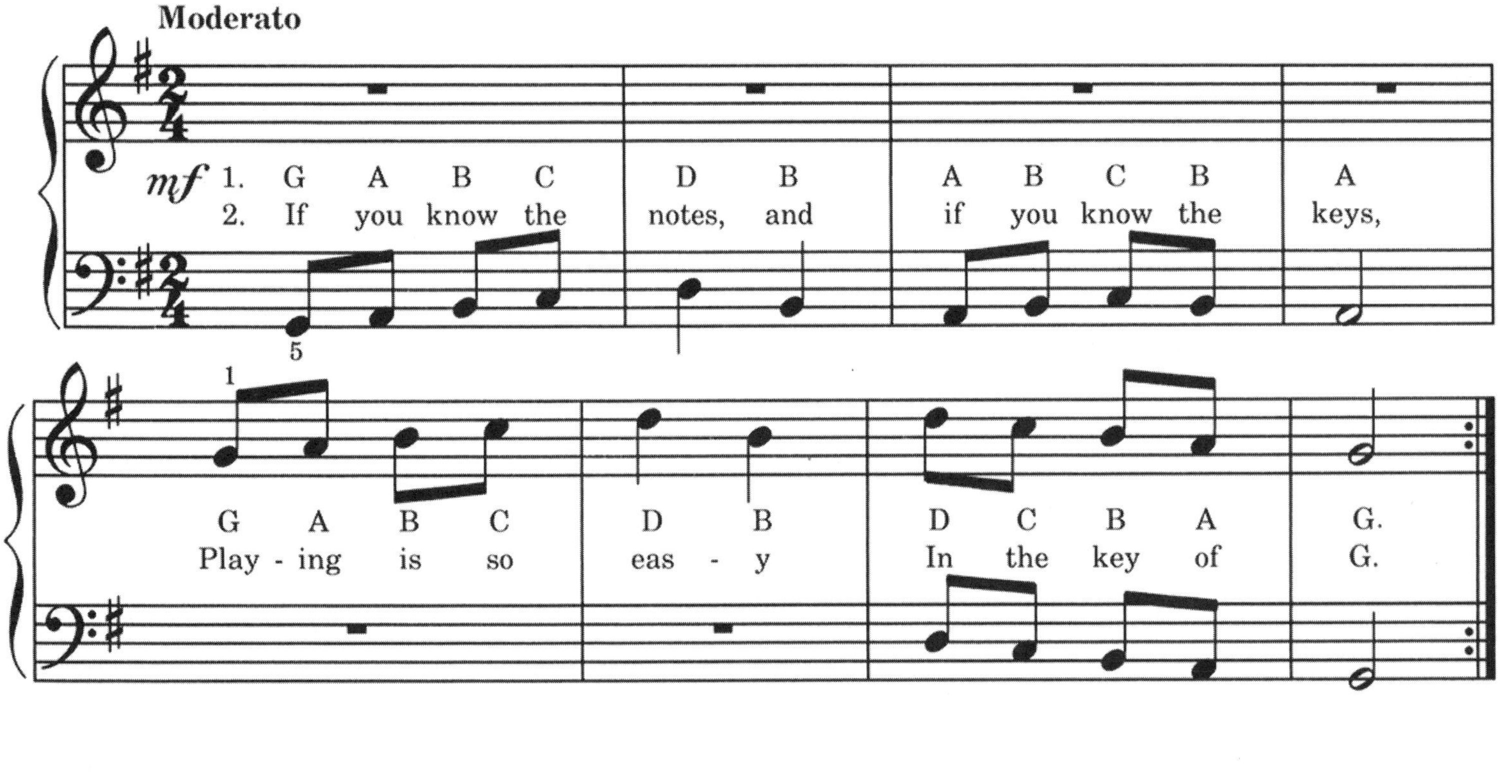

NATURAL SIGN

This ♮ is a NATURAL SIGN.
It cancels a sharp or flat.

MONDAY MORNING BLUES

GLOVER - STEWART

Andante (Walking tempo)

More Half Steps - Whole Steps

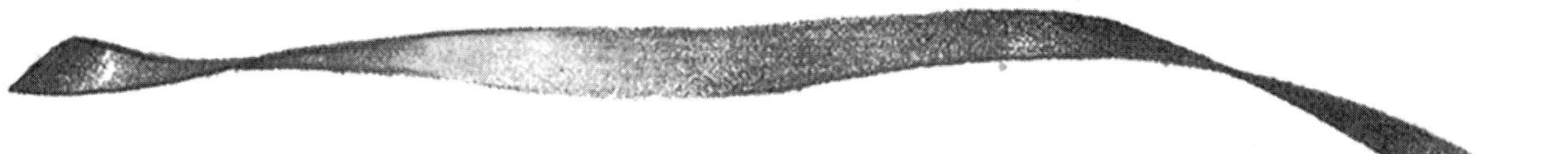

Under the following pairs of notes write H for half steps and W for whole steps.

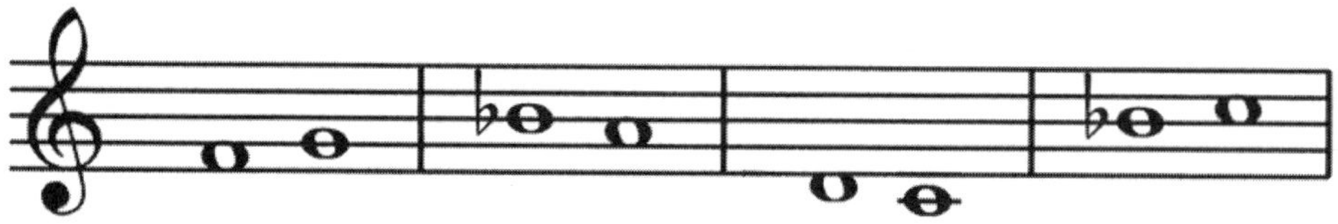

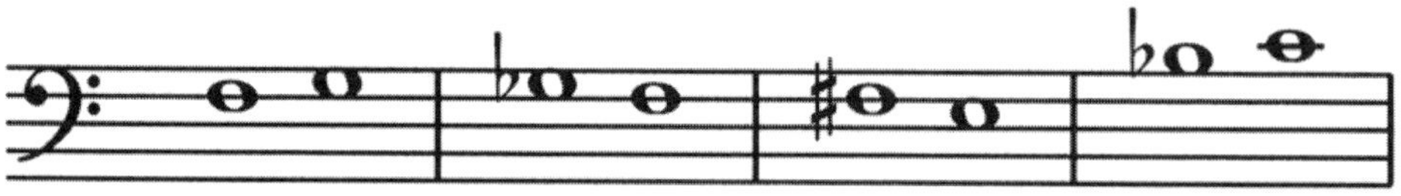

The notes that form the F Major Five Finger Position create a pattern of half and whole steps.

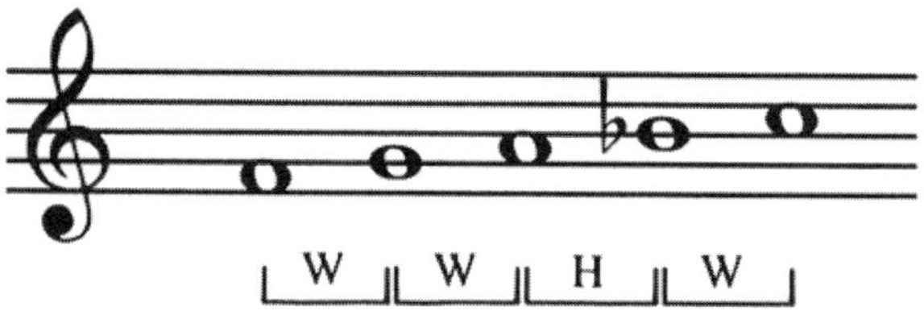

IMPORTANT: Notice that although the notes are different for each of the Major Five Finger Patterns below, the half and whole step pattern is the same.

Key of F Major

The key of F Major has one flat, B♭, placed at the beginning of each staff. This means all Bs are to be played flat. This is called the KEY SIGNATURE.

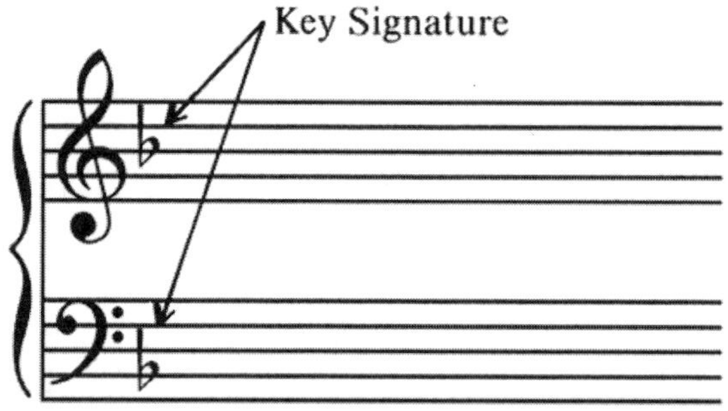

New Key - F Major

F MAJOR POSITION

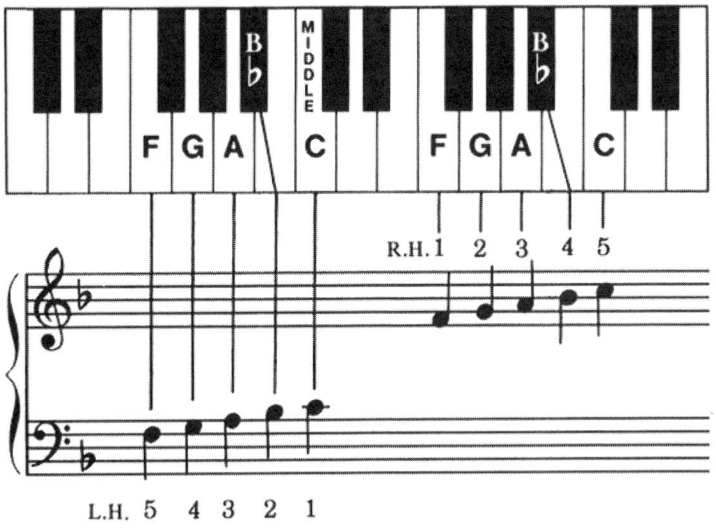

Key of ____________. Key signature ____________

AT EASE, PLEASE

Slowly

GLOVER - STEWART

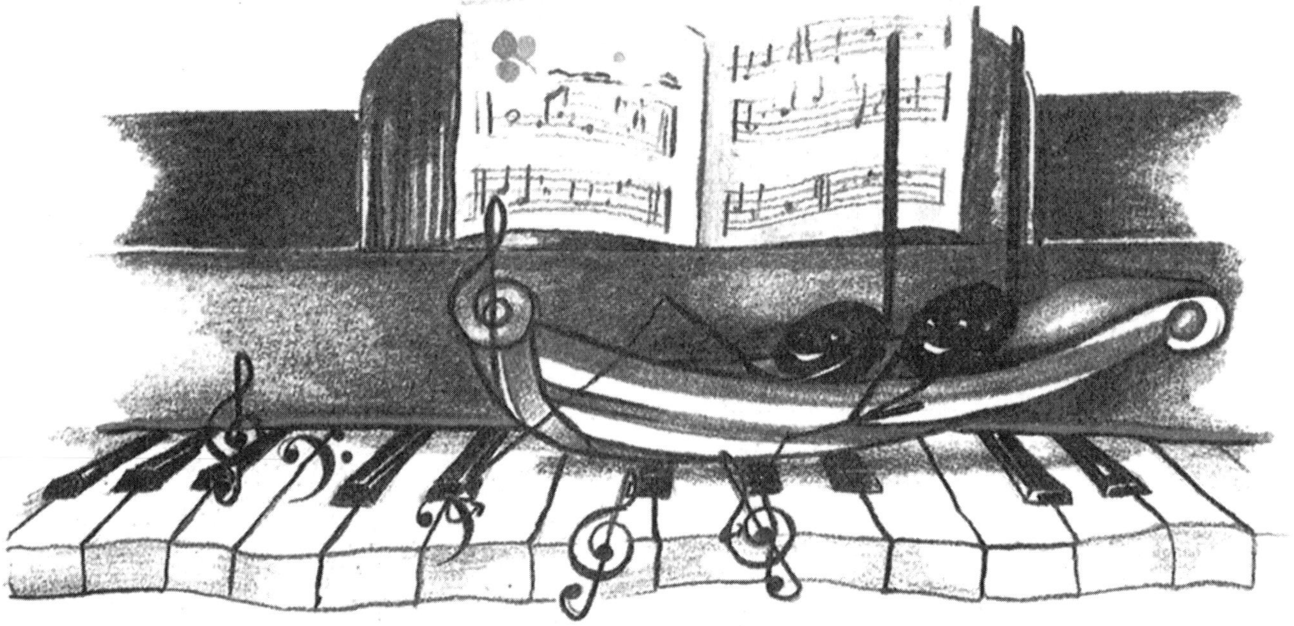

F POSITION FISHIN'

Allegretto

FOLK SONG

Andante means ____________

THE WINDMILL

(Tone Balance)

GLOVER - STEWART

EXPLORE: With both hands, tap the rhythm of this piece.

Do this activity with many other pieces in this book.

8va SIGN

The sign *8va* means to play one octave (8 keys) higher or lower than written.
When *8va* is placed above notes, play them one octave higher.
When *8va* is placed below notes, play them one octave lower.

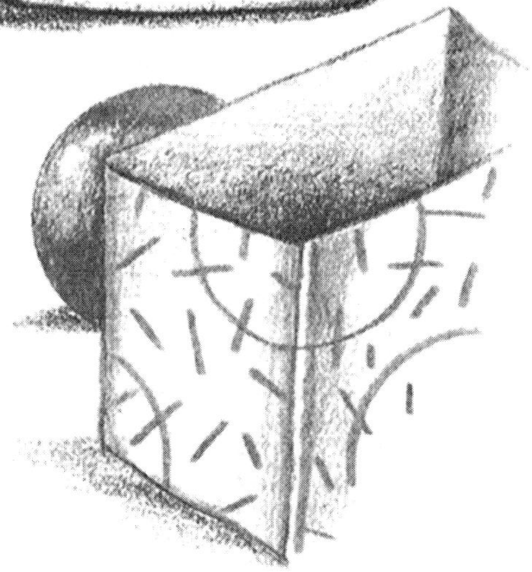

Practice this interval accompaniment before playing "The Mischievous Puppet."
Keep your eyes on the music. Do not look at your hands.

Key of ____________, Key Signature ____________

THE MISCHIEVOUS PUPPET

GLOVER - STEWART

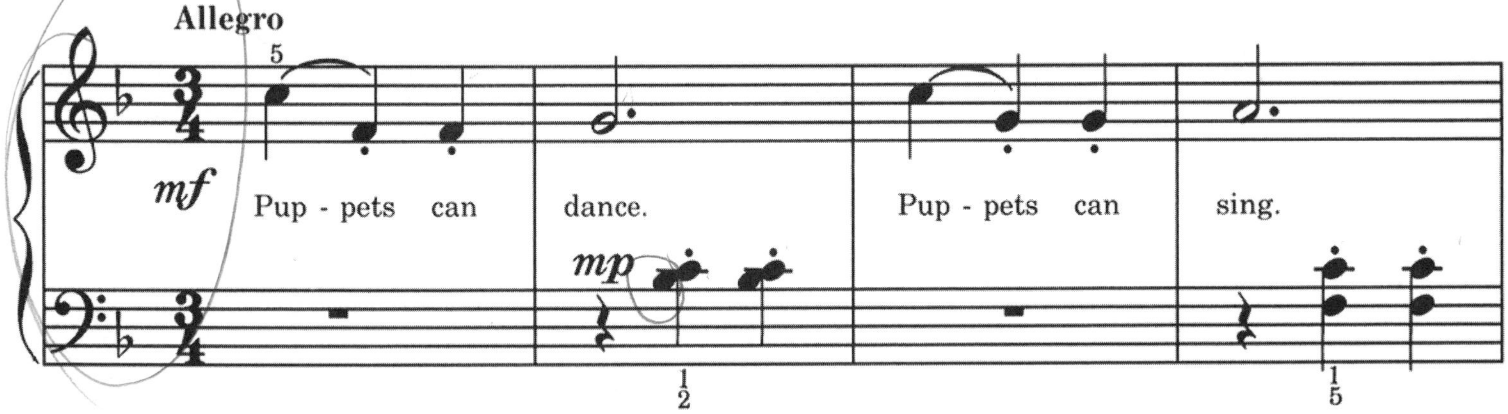

When a sharp or flat sign is placed before a note, it means to sharp or flat that note for the entire measure unless a natural sign is used.

Practice this interval accompaniment before playing "Sunny Day."
Keep your eyes on the music. Do not look at your hands.

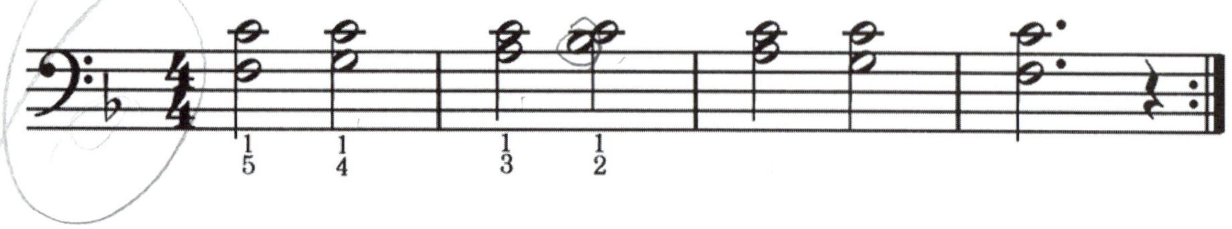

SUNNY DAY

GLOVER - STEWART

EXPLORE: As your teacher plays "Sunny Day", play the two highest Cs on the keyboard. Play the highest C with your right hand and the next highest C with your left hand using a quarter note pulse. Begin with your right hand.

YOU NAME IT!

TRADITIONAL

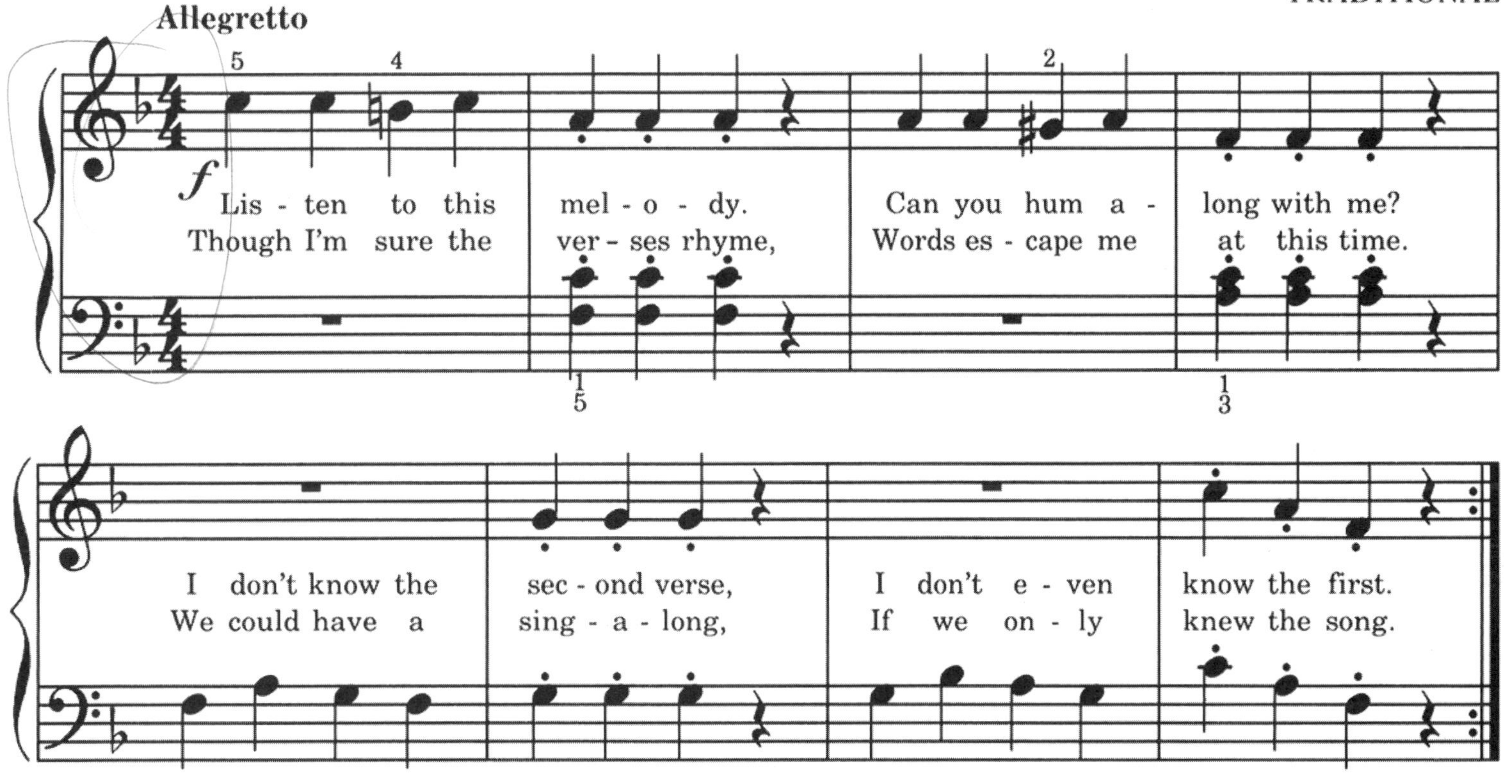

2. Do you think this song could be
One of these old melodies?
"Twinkle, Twinkle Little Star,
How I wonder what you are."?
"London Bridge Is Falling Down",
"Yankee Doodle Went To Town",
"Mary Had a Little Lamb",
"Jingle Bells" or "This Old Man"?

3. Wow, this song is getting worse
Every time we add a verse.
Every time we add a word,
Seems it's getting more absurd.
Maybe we should simply hum,
"Dum de dum de dum dum dum".
Well, I really did my best.
Up to you I'll leave the rest.

IMPORTANT!

TEACHER: It is recommended that TRANSPOSITION on pages 50-53, be presented at this time. It is also recommended that the student keep a list on page 54 of all songs transposed.

Franz Joseph Haydn (1732-1809), a famous Austrian composer, was recognized as a musical genius in his early childhood. His father, Matthias, was a fine tenor singer; his mother, Maria Koller, who had been a cook in the household of Count Harrach, was a choir singer. Of their twelve children, three became musicians. The gifted and talented Franz applied himself diligently to all study, whether singing, religion, counterpoint, violin or other instruments.

THEME FROM "THE SURPRISE SYMPHONY"

FRANZ JOSEPH HAYDN

Repeat both hands one octave higher

Changing Positions

Key of ______ Key signature ______

AU CLAIR DE LA LUNE

Moderato FOLK SONG

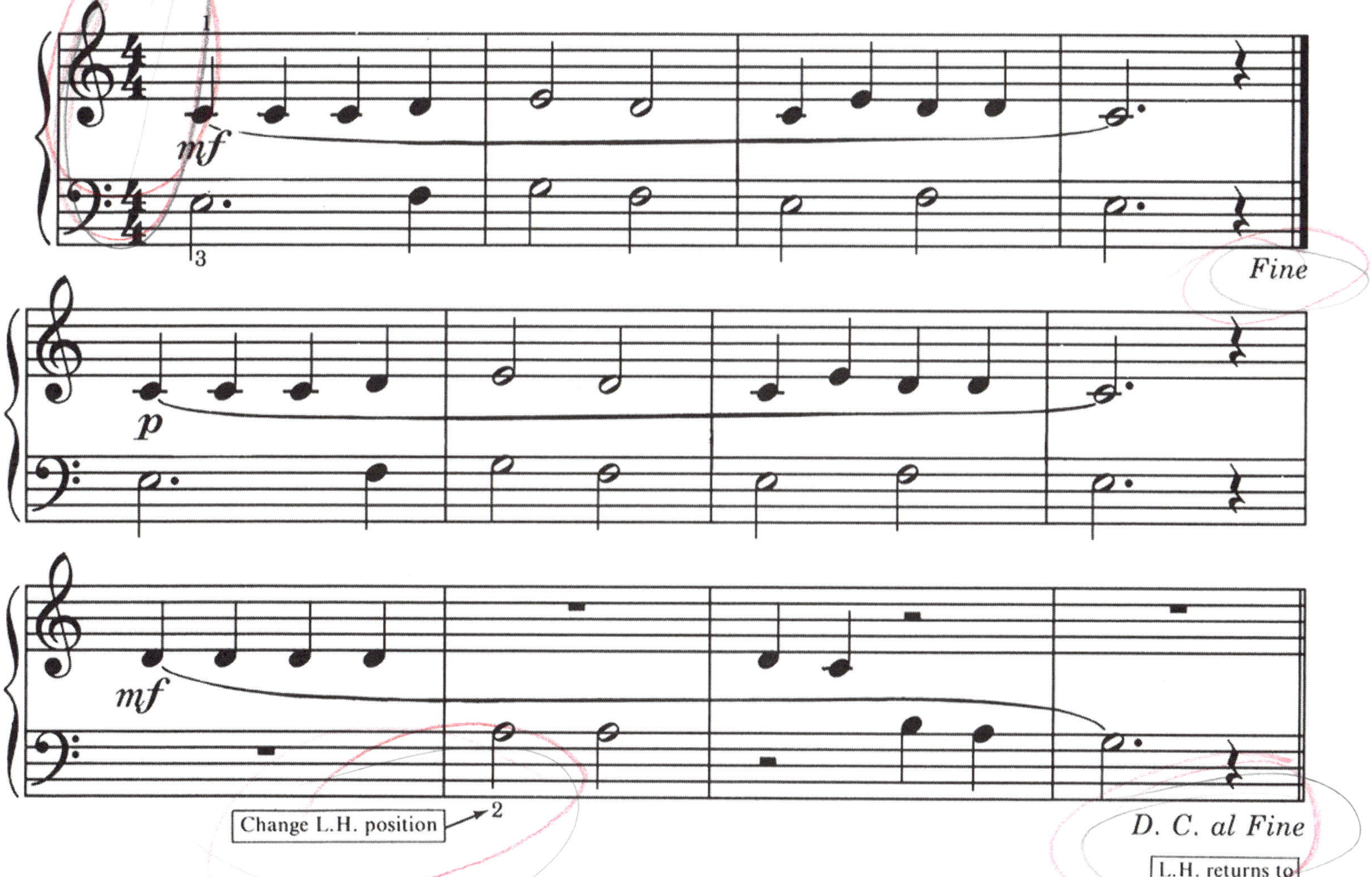

EXPLORE: Play, changing all Es to E flats.

Second Part (Student plays solo one octave higher)
Stems up - R.H.
Stems down - L.H.

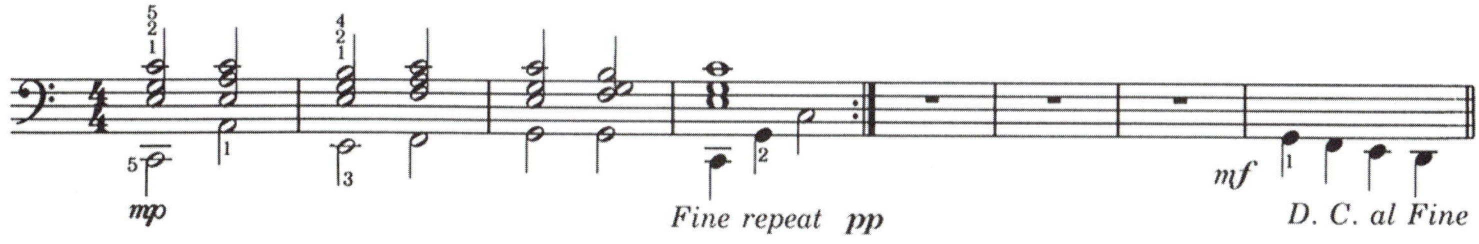

C, F AND G POSITIONS

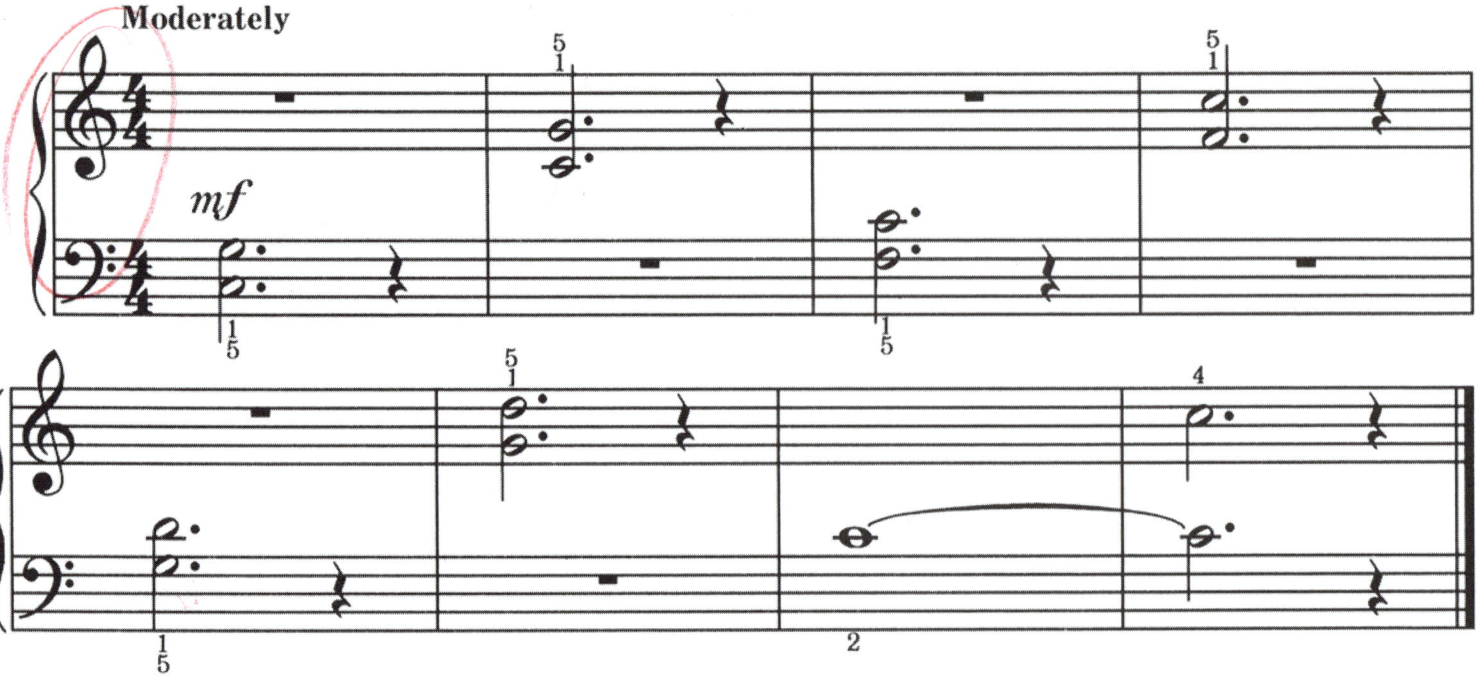

CHANGING PARTNERS

GLOVER - STEWART

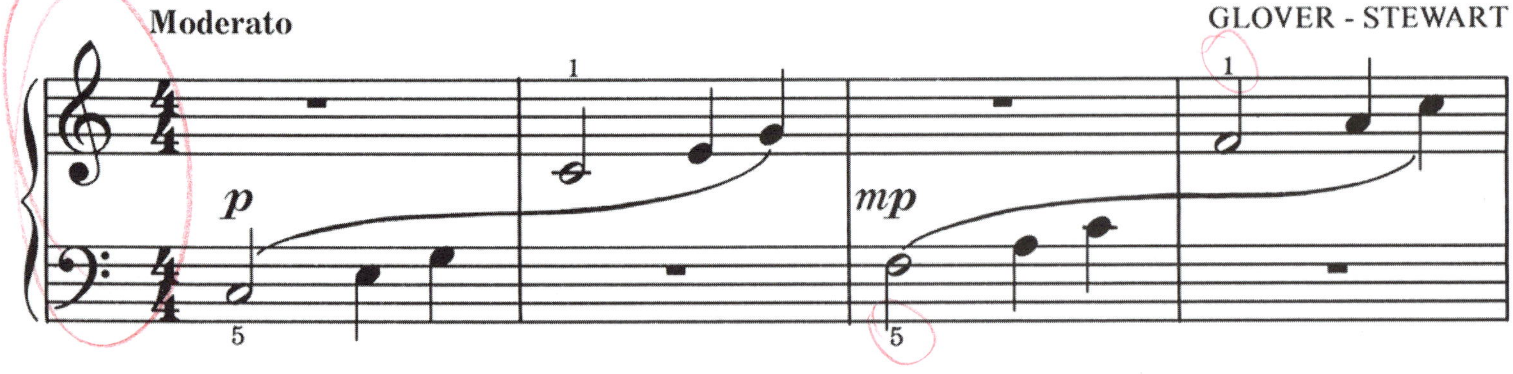

mf
p
mp
mf
p
R.H.
8va

ROCK IT!

C, F and G Positions

Move it!

GLOVER - STEWART

Damper Pedal

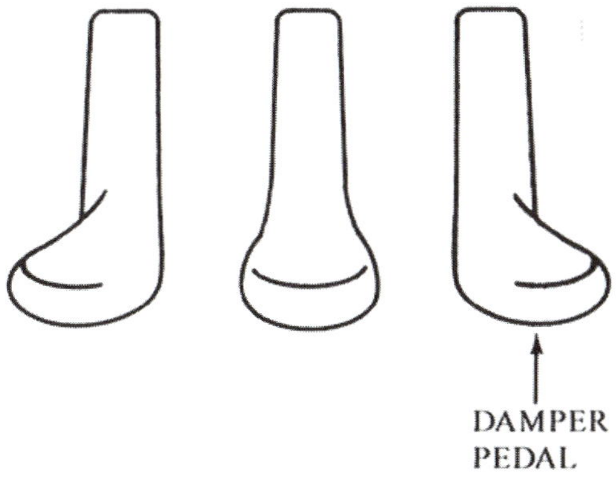

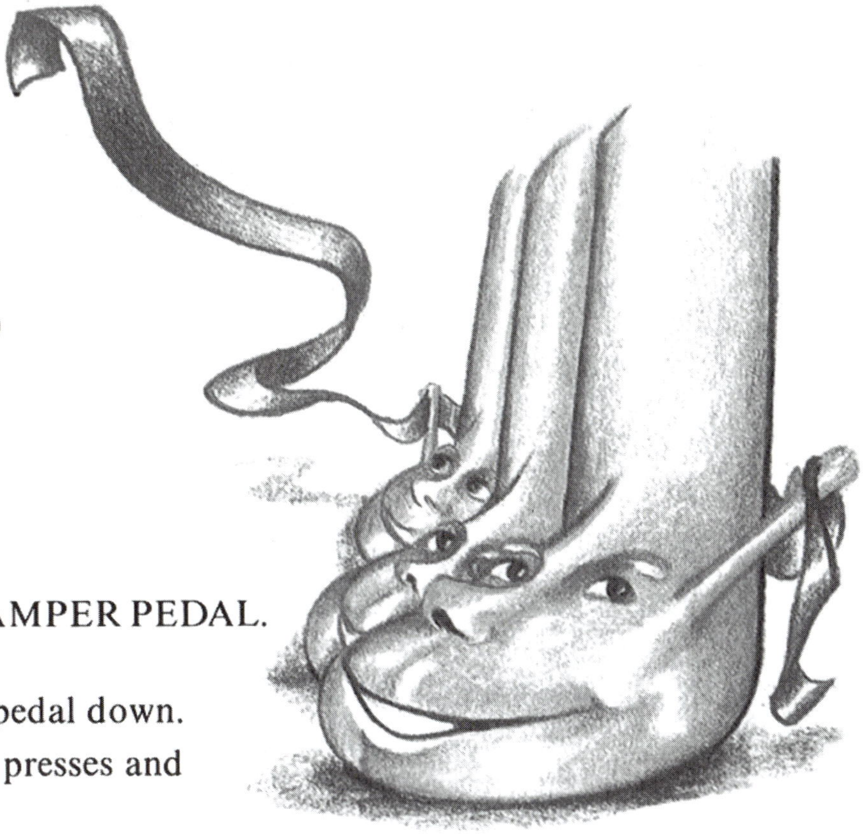

The pedal on the right side is called the DAMPER PEDAL. The DAMPER PEDAL sustains tones.

Use your right foot to press the damper pedal down.

Keep your heel on the floor as your foot presses and releases the pedal.

This is the pedal sign.

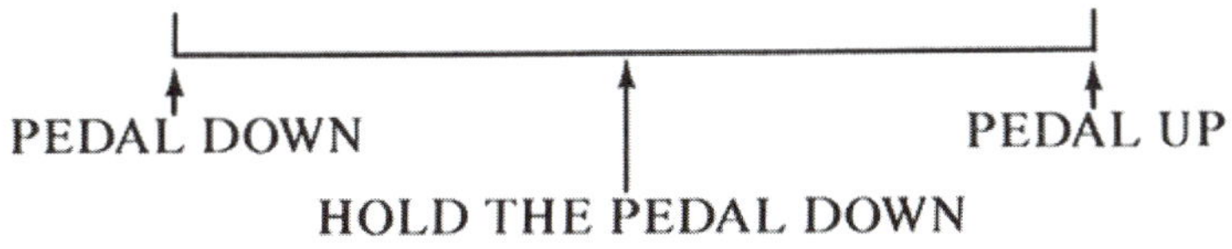

ALWAYS practice each piece WITHOUT the pedal until you can play the piece correctly. THEN you may add the pedal.

PEDAL ETUDE

An ETUDE is a piece for study or exercise.

Moderato

EXPLORE: Transpose "Pedal Etude" to the keys of F and G Major.

SHADOWS

Key of G. Key signature F#

Andante

GLOVER - STEWART

EXPLORE: Use your imagination to compose your own coda for this piece.

FORM IN MUSIC

MUSIC FORM is the pattern of a composition.
The patterns formed by the series of notes and rhythms may be alike, similar or different.

In this piece lines 1, 3 and 5 are alike.
Lines 2 and 4 are different.
How are lines 2 and 4 similar?

FOLK DANCE

FOLK MELODY

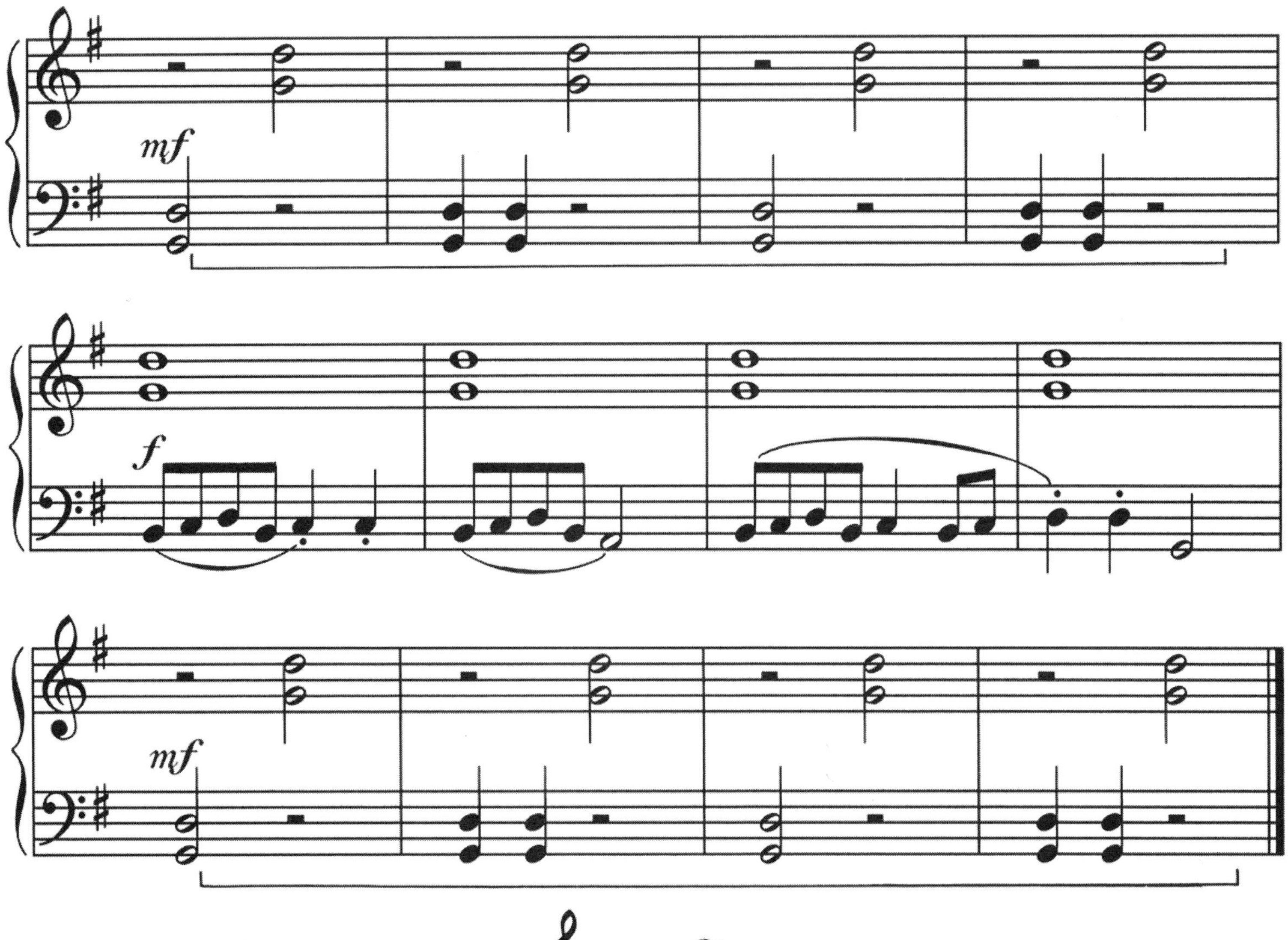

EXPLORE: With both hands (R.H. 𝄞 L.H. 𝄢) tap the rhythm of this piece.

CHRISTMAS MEDLEY

Secondo
(Teacher)

O Christmas Tree

TRADITIONAL

NEW POSITION

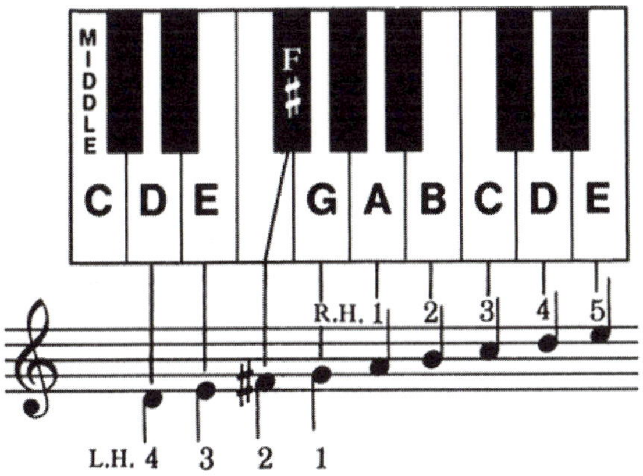

CHRISTMAS MEDLEY

Primo
(Student)

O Christmas Tree

TRADITIONAL

Secondo

Jolly Old Saint Nicholas

TRADITIONAL

NEW POSITION

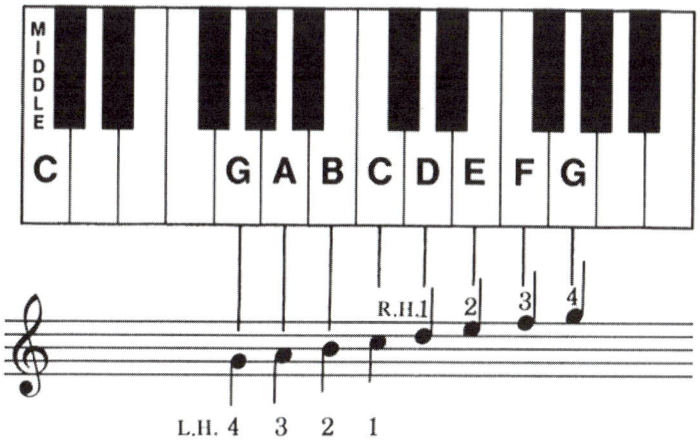

Primo

Jolly Old Saint Nicholas

TRADITIONAL

Transposition

Playing music in a key different from that in which it is written is called TRANSPOSING.

TRANSPOSING MELODIES

The following melody is shown three ways. First it is in the key of C Major, then TRANSPOSED into the keys of F Major and G Major. Play each melody.

C MAJOR

Notice the first note. It is C, the same as the key in which the melody is written. Also notice the intervals as the notes step up and down, then skip up and down, ending on C.

G MAJOR

Notice the first note. It is G, the same as the key in which the melody is written. Also notice the intervals as the notes step up and down, then skip up and down, ending on G.

F MAJOR

Notice the first note. It is F, the same as the key in which the melody is written. Also notice the intervals as the notes step up and down, then skip up and down, ending on F.

IMPORTANT: Notice that although the notes are different in all three keys, THE PATTERNS OF HALF STEPS, WHOLE STEPS AND OTHER INTERVALS ARE THE SAME.

1. Transpose this melody from C Major to G Major.
2. Play both melodies.

C Major

G Major

3. Transpose this melody from G Major to C Major.
4. Play both melodies.

G Major

C Major

5. Transpose this melody from F Major to G Major.
6. Play both melodies.

F Major

G Major

TRANSPOSING INTERVAL ACCOMPANIMENTS

7. Transpose the given intervals to the keys of G Major and F Major.

Key of ______ Major   Key of ______ Major   Key of ______ Major

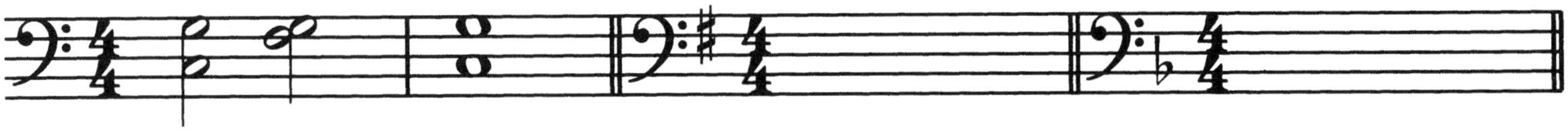

8. Transpose this melody and interval accompaniment from C Major to G Major or to F Major. Include the time signature and the correct key signature.

9. Play both melodies.

Many pieces in this book can be transposed from the original key to other keys.

As you transpose pieces, add their titles to the chart on page 54.

HOT CROSS BUNS

TRADITIONAL

1. Transpose "Hot Cross Buns" (page 52) from C Major to G Major. The first two measures are given.

2. Play.

HOT CROSS BUNS

TRADITIONAL

Allegro

1. Transpose "Hot Cross Buns" (page 52) from C Major to F Major. The first two measures are given.

2. Play.

HOT CROSS BUNS

TRADITIONAL

Allegro

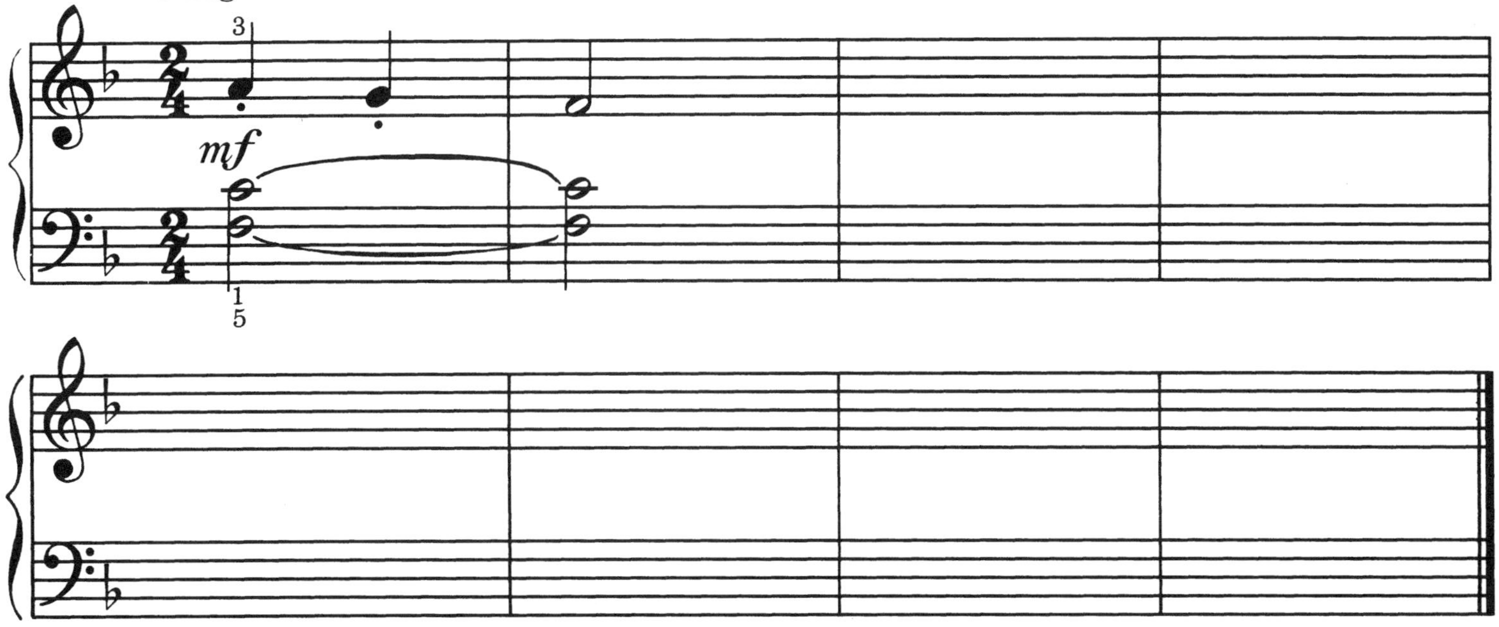

Pieces I Have Transposed

Title	Original Key	Transposed to the Key(s) of:

Review

1. Before each abbreviation or sign (Column 2), write the number of its correct name (Column 1).

1. Natural	______ *mf*
2. Piano	______ ♭
3. Diminuendo	______ *cresc.* <
4. Pedal (sign)	______ ***D.C. al Fine***
5. Mezzo piano	______ *mp*
6. Crescendo	______ ♯
7. Flat	______ *rit.*
8. Fermata	______ *8va*
9. Accent	______ *f*
10. Mezzo forte	______ *dim.* >
11. Sharp	______ *p*
12. Forte	______ └──┘
13. Slur	______ ♮
14. Ritardando	______ 𝄐
15. Da Capo al Fine	______ >
16. Octave (sign)	______ ⌒

2. Before each tempo mark (Column 2), write the number of its correct definition (Column 1).

1. Gradually slowing the tempo	______ **Moderato**
2. A moderate tempo	______ **Andante**
3. Rate of speed	______ **Adagio**
4. Slowly	______ **Allegretto**
5. A walking tempo	______ **Allegro**
6. Resume the original tempo	______ **A tempo**
7. Moderately fast tempo	______ ***rit.***
8. Fast, brisk tempo	______ **Tempo**

MUSIC DICTIONARY

MUSICAL TERM	ABBREVIATION or SIGN	DEFINITION
Accent Mark	>	Play the note louder
Adagio		Slow tempo
Allegretto		Moderately fast tempo
Allegro		Fast, brisk tempo
Andante		A walking tempo
A tempo		Resume the original tempo
Coda		An added ending
Crescendo	*cresc.* ＜	Play gradually louder
Da Capo al Fine	*D.C. al Fine*	Repeat from the beginning and play to the word "Fine" (pronounced "Fee-nay")
Damper Pedal		The pedal on the right side that sustains tones
Diminuendo	*dim.* ＞	Play gradually softer
Dynamic signs		Degrees of volume from soft to loud
Etude		A study piece or exercise
Fermata sign	𝄐	Hold the note or rest longer
Fine		The end (pronounced "Fee-nay")
Flat sign	♭	Lowers a note one half step
Forte	*f*	Loud
Half step		From one key to the very next key
Harmonic interval		Two tones sounded together
Incomplete measure		A measure with fewer counts than shown in the time signature
Interval		The distance between two tones
Key Signature		Sharps or flats written at the beginning of each staff to indicate the key in which a piece is written
Legato		Smooth and connected tones, usually indicated by a slur

MUSIC DICTIONARY

MUSICAL TERM	ABBREVIATION or SIGN	DEFINITION
Melodic interval		Two tones sounded separately
Mezzo forte	***mf***	Moderately loud
Mezzo piano	***mp***	Moderately soft
Moderato		A moderate tempo
Natural	♮	Cancels a sharp or flat
Octave sign	*8va*	Over notes: play one octave (8 keys) higher Under notes: play one octave (8 keys) lower
Pedal sign		Press, hold, then release the damper pedal
Phrase		A group of notes that form a musical sentence
Piano	***p***	Soft
Repeat sign	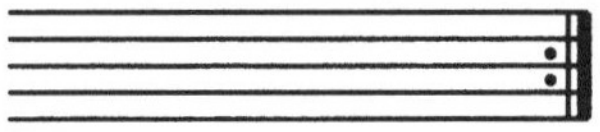	Indicates that a section is to be played again
Ritardando	rit.	Gradually slowing the tempo
Sharp sign	♯	Raises a note one half step
Slur		Indicates notes which are to be played legato
Staccato		Disconnected, detached tones
Tempo		Rate of speed
Tie		Connects one note to another note of the same letter name to combine their rhythmic values
Time signatures	$\frac{2}{4}$, $\frac{3}{4}$, $\frac{4}{4}$	The top number tells how many beats are in each measure. The bottom number tells which note receives one beat.
Upbeat		A note or notes played before the first full measure
Whole step		From one key to another key with one key in between

Certificate of Accomplishment

This certifies that

Emilie Durham

has completed

LESSONS,

LEVEL ONE

of the

David Carr Glover

METHOD for PIANO

and is promoted to **LEVEL TWO**

Jennie Durham

(Teacher)

5/11/15

(Date)